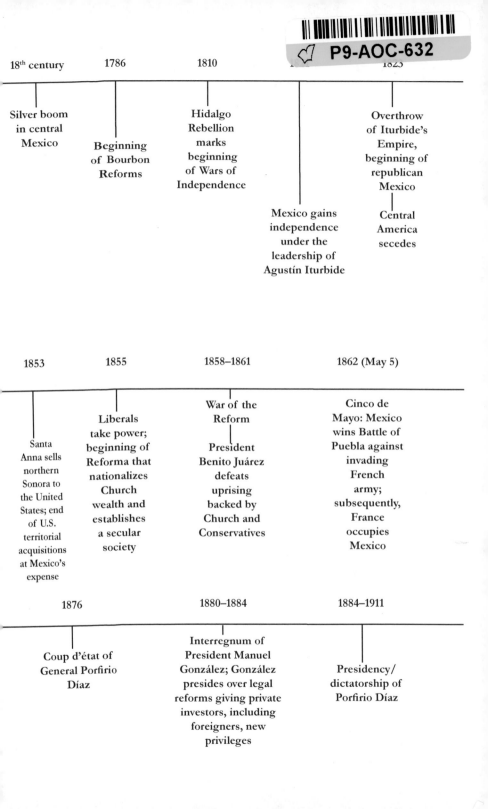

18th century	1786	1810	1823
Silver boom in central Mexico	Beginning of Bourbon Reforms	Hidalgo Rebellion marks beginning of Wars of Independence	Overthrow of Iturbide's Empire, beginning of republican Mexico
		Mexico gains independence under the leadership of Agustín Iturbide	Central America secedes

1853	1855	1858–1861	1862 (May 5)
		War of the Reform	Cinco de Mayo: Mexico wins Battle of Puebla against invading French army; subsequently, France occupies Mexico
Santa Anna sells northern Sonora to the United States; end of U.S. territorial acquisitions at Mexico's expense	Liberals take power; beginning of Reforma that nationalizes Church wealth and establishes a secular society	President Benito Juárez defeats uprising backed by Church and Conservatives	

1876	1880–1884	1884–1911
Coup d'état of General Porfirio Díaz	Interregnum of President Manuel González; González presides over legal reforms giving private investors, including foreigners, new privileges	Presidency/ dictatorship of Porfirio Díaz

Global History Series

KYLE LONGLEY, SERIES EDITOR

ARIZONA STATE UNIVERSITY

Jürgen Buchenau
University of North Carolina,
Charlotte

❧ Mexican Mosaic ☙
A Brief History
of Mexico

WILEY Blackwell

A John Wiley & Sons, Ltd., Publication

This edition first published 2008.
©2008 Harlan Davidson, Inc.

Harlan Davidson, Inc. was acquired by John Wiley & Sons in May 2012.

Registered Office
John Wiley & Sons Ltd, The Atrium, Southern Gate, Chichester, West Sussex, PO19 8SQ, UK

Editorial Offices
350 Main Street, Malden, MA 02148-5020, USA
9600 Garsington Road, Oxford, OX4 2DQ, UK
The Atrium, Southern Gate, Chichester, West Sussex, PO19 8SQ, UK

For details of our global editorial offices, for customer services, and for information about how to apply for permission to reuse the copyright material in this book please see our website at www.wiley.com/wiley-blackwell.

The right of Jürgen Buchenau to be identified as the author of this work has been asserted in accordance with the UK Copyright, Designs and Patents Act 1988.

Library of Congress Cataloging-in-Publication Data

Buchenau, Jürgen, 1964–
  Mexican mosaic : a brief history of Mexico / Jürgen Buchenau.— 1st ed.
        p. cm.— (Global history series)
Includes bibliographical references and index.
  ISBN-13: 978-0-88295-263-5 (alk. paper)
  1. Mexico—History. I. Title.
  F1226.B83 2008
  972—dc22
                                2008002889

Cover illustration: "The Epic of American Civilization" a 24-panel work by Mexican Mural Renaissance painter Jose Clemente Orozco (1883-1949). Featured, Panel 16 "Hispano-America"; left, portion of Panel 15 "Anglo-America"; right, portion of Panel 17 "Gods of the Modern World." This expressionist piece illustrates the history of the Americas from the arrival of the Aztecs into central Mexico to the development of modern industrialism. The 3,200 square foot mural is located in the reserve corridor of Dartmouth College's Baker Library. Photograph by Leonardo Fotos.
Cover design: Christopher Calvetti, c2it graphics

To my father,
Helmut Buchenau

¶ Editor's Foreword ☙

*F*or Americans, no country's society, and by extension history, has been more actively integrated with their own than that of Mexico. The closest and most populous neighbor of the United States, Mexico daily affects Americans—economically, culturally, and politically. Likewise, the United States shapes Mexico. Over the course of two centuries, the relationship between the two nations has often been ambivalent, even contentious, but always significant.

Mexican Mosaic: A Brief History of Mexico, the second volume in Harlan Davidson's Global History Series, provides readers with a concise, accessible, and highly affordable survey history of the subject nation, with an emphasis on its active role in the global community. Jürgen Buchenau has succeeded admirably in carrying out a challenging task: conveying the complex history of Mexico in a comprehensive but lively narrative, one spanning five centuries from Conquest, through Colonial, Revolutionary, Modern, and present-day Mexico. In the pages that follow, students will gain a practical understanding of the major trends in the nation's economic, political, cultural, and social development and an appreciation of Mexico's relationships with all global powers—not simply the "Colossus of the North."

There has long been a need for such a book, and *Mexican Mosaic* will serve as a useful tool to instructors who teach a variety of courses ranging from the History of Mexico to the Latin American survey, to the Caribbean World, the Atlantic World, World History, and Comparative Global Civilization.

It is my hope that students of all levels with enjoy and benefit from reading this important new volume (as well as the first on Cuba and forthcoming ones) as they learn about and begin to ponder our world—past, present, and future—and their place in it.

Kyle Longley
Snell Family Dean's
Distinguished Professor of History
Arizona State University

☙ Contents ❧

❧ Acknowledgments ☙

T his book would not have been possible without the help of friends, colleagues, and family. Above all, I appreciate the support, encouragement, and patience of the publisher, Andrew J. Davidson, and the series editor, Kyle Longley. My original inspiration for writing a short textbook came in the spring of 1987 in Gilbert Joseph's History of Mexico course. Gil's ability to make sense of the vast complexity of Mexican history in one short semester convinced me of the need for a brief text that would allow instructors to assign more secondary material such as primary sources, articles, and monographs. Among many other things, this book is a tribute to Gil's teaching and mentorship.

Most of all, I thank all Mexicans with whom I have had the privilege of interacting over the past three decades, both in Mexico and in the United States. Every trip south of the Rio Grande has been a learning opportunity, a humbling experience even after twenty years of research in Mexican archives and libraries. Collectively, these trips allowed me to take the photographs reproduced in this book.

Students in two separate History of Mexico classes at UNC Charlotte in the spring of 2005 and the fall of 2006 contributed to the writing of this book by commenting on existing texts and by sharing their viewpoints on what makes a good textbook. By encouraging me to focus on a few important themes, these students helped me conquer my own reservations about an exercise that necessarily overgeneralizes in the extreme in condensing the long and complex history of a socially and ethnically diverse nation in a brief text. Two of my colleagues at UNC Charlotte, Lyman Johnson and Angela Herren, provided valuable advice on the first chapter. The chapter on the

xi

Mexican Revolution reflects countless hours of discussions with Greg Crider of Wingate University. The encouragement of friends was also of vital importance. Among those who have inspired me in the writing of this book, I particularly recognize Tom Cole and Sensei Michael Price.

Finally, I could not have written this book without my family; both the gran familia in Germany and Mexico and the nuclear family in Charlotte. As a descendant of German-Mexicans, I have always carried a piece of Mexico inside me, and I consider myself lucky to have been able to nurture that aspect of my identity. Anabel, Nicolas, and Julia are enthusiastic fellow travelers who enjoy Mexico as much as I do. They make all my efforts worthwhile.

Charlotte, North Carolina
October 2007

¶ Introduction ✿

July 3, 2006. It is a cool Monday morning in Mexico City. A street peddler has just set up shop on a sidewalk in front of a bank building on the posh Paseo de la Reforma, the famous French-style boulevard commissioned by the Austrian-born Emperor Maximilian and his wife Carlota in the 1860s. The peddler is sitting on a large hand-woven shawl in order to stay warm on the cold concrete, and she uses another one to display her wares: batteries, toys, and CDs, all made in Asia. Yet another shawl slung around her neck cradles a baby whose dark eyes peek out to gaze up at the tall bank building. Men and women in expensive suits hurry by with newspapers tucked under their arms. The papers proclaim that the presidential election of the previous day has resulted in a virtual tie between Felipe Calderón Hinojosa, candidate of the conservative ruling party, the Partido Acción Nacional (National Action Party, or PAN), and Andrés Manuel López Obrador, the left-leaning former mayor of Mexico City and candidate of the Partido de la Revolución Democrática (Party of the Democratic Revolution, or PRD). A preliminary vote count has Calderón ahead by 1 percent, or 377,000 votes. A third candidate, Roberto Madrazo of the Partido Revolucionario Institucional (Institutional Revolutionary Party, or PRI) has placed a distant third, only six years after his party lost a presidential election for the first time since the Great Depression. Worried that the political uncertainty will lead to trouble on the stock market, the pedestrians in suits scarcely take notice of the street peddler, who makes about one hundred pesos, or $9 U.S., on a very good day. Politically, she supports López Obrador, who campaigned under the motto *"por el bien de todos, primero los pobres"* ("for the good of everyone, the poor people first"). "If Andrés Manuel doesn't win," she says, "it will be because of fraud! And it wouldn't be the

1

first time," she proclaims, referring to the 1988 presidential election that her party lost only after a mysterious "crash" of the computer system that tallied the votes. After decades of the authoritarian rule of one single party, in which the outcome of elections was never in doubt, our conversation now highlights Mexico's volatile transition to democracy during the last twenty years.

The scene conjures up the country's enduring contradictions, what historian Lesley Byrd Simpson has called the "many Mexicos." Indeed, the country's stunning geographical, ethnic, and social diversity defies efforts at historical generalization. Focused primarily on the period since independence in 1821, this brief survey cannot possibly do justice to such a rich history. Instead, it will only delineate some of the major processes that have taken place at the national level while hinting at regional and local countercurrents, or exceptions from larger trends. Due to its brevity, this book focuses on political and economic history, although anecdotes and brief biographical sketches will give readers a sense of social and cultural history—particularly how ordinary Mexicans lived their history.

Intended as a brief introduction to Mexican history, this text emphasizes two major themes as organizing principles: Mexico in the global community and the negotiation of power. In keeping with the overarching purpose of the Global History Series, the following chapters analyze the way Mexicans interacted with the United States and the rest of the outside world. As President Porfirio Díaz, who dominated Mexico from 1876 to 1911, once purportedly remarked: "Poor Mexico: so far from God, and so close to the United States." As political leaders, soldiers, consumers, entrepreneurs, and migrants—indeed, in all aspects of their lives—Mexican men and women have increasingly confronted global influences, and especially the cultural, economic, and political presence of their northern neighbor. The book's second theme analyzes the way Mexicans have contested and negotiated their place in a society marked by great social differences, limited access to political power and impartial justice, and repeated upheaval. What might be called the "great wars and revolutions" of Mexican history—the conquest (1519–21), the Wars of Independence (1810–21), the foreign interventions and civil wars of the nineteenth century, and the revolution of 1910 revealed the instability of a power structure in Mexico dominated by a wealthy minority. Interrupting extended periods of apparent quiescence, these upheavals also manifested the multiple ways in which ordinary Mexicans challenged and modified this existing power structure. Against the homogenizing forces of globalization, local and regional identities remain strong. This is the enduring paradox of Mexico's complex and diverse society.

A DIVERSE NATION

Mexico is the fifth-largest country in the Americas, behind Canada, the United States, Brazil, and Argentina. Its territory is one-fourth that of the United States. Located between 14 and 32° north and 87 and 117° west, it encompasses both subtropical and tropical latitudes as well as three time zones (not counting the state of Sonora, which, like its U.S. neighbor, Arizona, does not follow daylight-savings time). Geographically, it forms part of both North and Central America. Mexico borders three countries: the United States, Belize, and Guatemala; and three seas: the Gulf of Mexico and the Caribbean to the east and north, and the Pacific Ocean in the west and south.

Mountains define much of the Mexican landscape; once the Spanish conquistador Hernán Cortés balled up a sheet of paper and unfolded it to demonstrate to his superiors the nature of the land he had conquered. Two impressive mountain ranges, the Sierra Madre Occidental and the Sierra Madre Oriental, traverse northern and central Mexico, and a volcanic belt runs from Colima in the west to Orizaba in the east. This belt—the Sierra Volcánica Transversal—features the country's highest mountains, all over sixteen thousand feet: the Ixtaccíhuatl and Popocatépetl southeast of Mexico City, and the Pico de Orizaba between the states of Puebla and Veracruz. In the south, the Isthmus of Tehuantepec, a stretch of lowlands in Veracruz and Oaxaca, provides the only place in Mexico where goods can easily be shipped overland from the Gulf to the Pacific. Even farther east, the Sierra Madre del Sur separates the peninsula of Yucatán from the Pacific coast and runs into Central America, before ending in eastern Costa Rica. These mountains contribute to the creation of several distinct climatic zones and thousands of microclimates that make Mexico's flora and fauna among the most varied in the entire world. These climatic zones are defined primarily by altitude and rainfall: the arid north, the temperate and cool center, the humid tropical Gulf Coast, the dry tropical Pacific Coast, and the rainforests of Chiapas. The steep slopes of the mountains and the great disparities in precipitation pose challenges to human settlement. Intense struggles over land and water have marked Mexican history, and even today, only 10 percent of the country's territory is under cultivation. Likewise, Mexico's topography has always made the building of infrastructure such as roads and railways a monumental task.

This variegated landscape, however, encouraged a strong sense of regionalism. Before the Spanish conquest, Mesoamerica was home to a variety of indigenous civilizations. Spanish colonial rule transformed rather than eliminated regionally and locally based indigenous traditions and cultures. Many

Mexicans still feel a deep allegiance to their region as the *patria chica*, or little fatherland, and the efforts at forging a strong nation-state remain incomplete. In some cases, the patria chica coincided with an entire state, such as in the small states of Aguascalientes and Tlaxcala, but most of the states featured strong local rivalries within that further complicated the regional picture. At present, there are thirty-two states in Mexico, in addition to a federal district, the heart of the Mexico City metropolitan area. Having 22 million people, greater Mexico City is one of the three largest cities in the world, and it continues to register a disproportionate impact on the rest of Mexico. The inhabitants of the capital, labeled *chilangos* by the rest of the nation, have long enjoyed the reputation of looking down at their fellow Mexicans from the "provinces." In fact, however, Mexico has several other large and influential cities: Guadalajara, with 5 million inhabitants, and Monterrey, León, and Puebla, all with well over 1 million. The struggle of regional and local actors to shape and contest the overweening influence of the national capital is one of the enduring themes in Mexican history.

The 2006 presidential election was a prime example of regional disparities. According to the official vote count, López Obrador dominated in the south, racking up 58 percent of the vote in Mexico City, or more than twice as much as Calderón, and even larger margins in Tabasco and Oaxaca. However, the PAN candidate won big in the north, particularly in the conservative central state of Guanajuato, where he obtained 59 percent of the vote, almost four times as much as López Obrador.

Mexico has a large and ethnically diverse population. At 105 million inhabitants according to the 2000 census, the country trails only the United States and Brazil in population among the American nations. In addition, more than 20 million Mexicans and their descendants live in the United States and Canada. There are more Spanish speakers in Mexico than in any other country of the world. However, the country is also home to more than 30 million indigenous people, many of whom speak a language other than Spanish as their native tongue. Often referred to as "Indians"—a term that reflects Christopher Columbus's mistaken belief that the explorer had landed in India during his first trip to the Americas—indigenous Mexicans use more than fifty different languages and dialects. Among the most important of these languages are Náhuatl, spoken in central Mexico, and the various Maya languages of the Yucatán Peninsula and the southeastern state of Chiapas. Many of these languages have even made their way into the United States by way of immigration; for example, sizable Mixtec and Nahua communities thrive in Los Angeles and other cities. Most of the Spanish-speaking majority of Mexicans are *mestizos*, or people of mixed ethnic descent. The ancestry of the mestizos combines indigenous, European, and African elements. Only a small minority—approximately 5 percent—is of European, predominantly Spanish, origin.

The economy of Mexico is as diverse as the land and its people. In general terms, the country numbers among the nations of the "developing world," or in the rhetoric that has survived from the Cold War, the "Third World." In 2006, the per capita GNP, adjusted for purchasing power, stood at just over $10,600, or one-fourth of that of the United States. That figure was slightly above the world average. On the strength of its economy, based on industrial production, agriculture, mining, tourism, and the remittances from abroad of millions of migrant workers, Mexico numbers among the more prosperous nations of the developing world. In the last decade, Mexican exporters have benefited from the North American Free Trade Agreement (NAFTA) and the General Agreement on Tariffs and Trade (GATT). These agreements have slashed import tariffs in the United States and other developed nations and given producers greater access to consumers around the world. In Latin America, only Argentina, Chile, and Costa Rica feature a significantly higher per capita GNP, and that in Brazil is 15 percent lower. Guatemala's per capita GNP weighs in at $4,900, or less than half of Mexico's, and Honduras' and Nicaragua's stand at a scant $3,000.

Yet these raw numbers do not reveal the unequal distribution of wealth. Mexico boasts the second-highest number of millionaires in the world (behind the United States). In its 2007 ranking, *Forbes Magazine* listed telecom tycoon Carlos Slim Helu as the world's third wealthiest individual, with a net worth of $49 billion. Since then, he has overtaken Warren Buffett and only trails Bill Gates. Unlike these two North Americans, Slim does not give generously to charities, arguing that his wealth supports job creation. Apart from Slim and the rest of the rich, a sizable middle class enjoys amenities much like its counterparts in Europe and the United States. At the other end of the social spectrum, more than half of all Mexicans are destitute, and the minimum wage is $4 per day. Thirty million Mexicans subsist on less than $2 per day. High population growth has produced more workers than the economy can absorb; by one estimate, one of every three Mexicans is under the age of fifteen. There is also a growing regional disparity of income. While the industrializing zones of northern Mexico and tourist enclaves such as Cancún and Cozumel have benefited from NAFTA and greater integration into the world economy, much of the heavily indigenous south of the nation has fallen behind due to its agricultural base. As a result, millions of people have moved north of the border in search of a better life, and others have taken drastic steps to seek redress for their plight. For example, on January 1, 1994—the same day NAFTA took effect—a rebellion broke out in Chiapas. Led by the enigmatic Subcomandante Marcos, the Zapatista rebellion recalled Emiliano Zapata, who led an army of *campesinos* (peasants) in the Mexican Revolution of 1910, with demands of land reform and social justice. The movement highlighted the campesinos' enduring struggle to reclaim land taken from them by large agribusinesses, and to ensure freedom and social justice for all.

MEXICO AND THE WORLD

As the foregoing discussion indicates, Mexico is a nation in close contact with the rest of the world. Its border with the United States—the object of much recent controversy regarding Mexican immigration—is the longest between a developed and a developing country. Since the 1500s, Mexico—first as a colony of Spain and, after 1821, as an independent nation—has exported thousands of tons of silver, affecting currencies and prices as far away as China and India. In the century following independence, Mexico was invaded six times, once by Spain, twice by France, and three times by the United States, which annexed half of the country's territory in the mid-nineteenth century. Since then, Mexico has played an ever more important part in the world economy, providing precious metals and oil, among other commodities, as well as many manufactured products. The country is an important tourist destination today, and consumer culture—particularly that of the U.S. variety—has made a permanent home there. Mexicans consume as many soft drinks per capita as do North Americans; affluent youngsters own iPods and PlayStations, and despite (or perhaps because of) the existence a network of public transportation, cars are as much a status symbol in Mexico as in the United States. There is a flip side to this ever-growing integration into a global economy and culture. Only the upper and middle classes can afford most of the products advertised on TV. And, unfortunately, Mexico also plays an influential role in the production and transportation of illegal drugs, many of which end up north of the border.

This increasing engagement with the rest of the world over five centuries has slowly forged a nation out of the patchwork of indigenous, mestizo, and Spanish peoples, as well as regional and local cultures. Since the Spanish conquest, flows of people, commodities, and cultural practices have gradually created an imagined national community as part of a global system. Over time, more and more Mexicans have participated in the imagining of this community. Despite the great differences among them, the street peddler and the business executives, López Obrador, Calderón, and Subcomandante Marcos all identify themselves as Mexicans. They borrow freely from the world, only to Mexicanize their imports: Spanish-language rap blasts out of car windows, spaghetti sauce has just a hint of spicy peppers, and Mexicans have developed their own versions of soap operas and reality shows. At the same time, Mexican culture has gone international: Corona beer is available in the bars of New York and Berlin, Mexican restaurants can be found in any American suburb as well as Sydney and Paris, and immigration has produced hybrid cultures in the United States. Mexican *telenovelas* (soap operas) such as *Ugly Betty* are as popular in the United States as in Mexico, and the Ballet Folklórico performs regional folk dances at concert halls across the globe. Thus national identity serves as an important connection between local practice and global structure. In the words of the author Carlos Monsiváis: "the Mexican assimilates [foreign culture] without being assimilated."

Over the last century, Mexico has played a significant role in world affairs. It was home to the first social revolution of the twentieth century, and the revolutionary Constitution of 1917 was the first such document to attempt to defend a nation against foreign economic exploitation. After World War II, the country assumed a position of leadership in the developing world and emerged as a significant oil-producing and industrializing nation. As a result, the Mexican government has not always followed the lead of the United States, criticizing U.S. intervention in Cuba and Central America and, most recently, the war in Iraq. If Mexico depends more than ever on the United States, the reverse also applies.

This book is divided into five short chapters. Chapter One analyzes the indigenous, Spanish, and African antecedent peoples as well as their fusion into a new mix of cultures during the colonial period (1519–1810). Chapter Two tells the story of Mexico's Wars of Independence and the troubled beginning of the new nation amidst civil wars, foreign invasions, and economic stagnation (1810–67). Chapter Three describes the era of liberal modernization (1867-1910) that brought a measure of political stability and economic growth but also dictatorship and unprecedented social inequality. Chapter Four delineates the Mexican Revolution (1910–46), inaugurated by a broad-based movement that sought to bring redress for these problems, and ended in the establishment of an official revolutionary party. Finally, Chapter Five surveys the period since World War II, an era marked by the dominance and eventual demise of the PRI, mass migration to the United States, and ever closer ties with the outside world. At the end of the book, a bibliographical essay provides a starting point for those who want a more detailed understanding of Mexico's long and complex history.

If I see the street peddler again the next time I am in Mexico, I plan to ask her about Andrés Manuel. In September 2006, the federal elections jury—the Tribunal Federal Electoral—declared Calderón the winner of the presidential election by a narrow margin of less than 300,000 votes. Alleging massive fraud, Calderón's opponent, López Obrador, did not concede, rallying the masses in the Zócalo, or main square of Mexico City. In protest, his supporters paralyzed the Paseo de la Reforma for weeks by constructing a vast tent city on the lanes and sidewalks of the sprawling boulevard.

By now (2007) the tents are long gone, and Calderón has been sworn in as the new president, but López Obrador and his supporters still do not recognize the triumph of the PAN. Leading a parallel government, they hold out hope for their vision of Mexico—a vision quite different from that of Calderón and his conservative allies. Hence, although one might find Coca Cola as surely in a remote indigenous village as in a Mexico City mall, Mexico remains a complex mosaic of competing and coexisting cultures and viewpoints. The chapters that follow tell the story of how this mosaic came to be.

CHAPTER ONE

❧ The Making of Mexico ❧

*T*o the people who had just landed on the coast, it was called the year 1519. Already there were ominous signs in the Aztec Empire, a land that stretched from the Pacific to the Atlantic. The inhabitants of the capital city, Tenochtitlán, were restless. There had been crop failures and droughts, as well as wars with neighboring indigenous communities. But none of these worries compared with the news that light-skinned people had disembarked on the coast several hundred miles east of Tenochtitlán, men who appeared to possess miraculous powers. They were mounted on animals much larger than any the Aztecs (or *Mexica*, as they called themselves) had ever seen. The invaders carried weapons that emitted smoke, fire, and enormous noise and killed people standing hundreds of feet away. They wore iron armor, shields, and hats, and they spoke in a language none of the indigenous people had ever heard. A year later, yet another Spanish expedition arrived, bringing more disruption to the indigenous world. Some of these newcomers were not as light skinned as the others—in fact, their skin appeared so dark that those who witnessed the explorers dubbed them "gods of the earth." And sickness followed the second expedition. Only days after the arrival of the newcomers, some of the natives who had come into contact with them contracted smallpox, a disease they had never known before, which proved fatal to many. The invaders were still many days' journeys away, but they carried ill portents. Little did the Aztecs know that the days of their empire were numbered, and that the invasion would produce mass death, the destruction of their way of life, and the forging of what the twentieth-century Mexican intellectual José Vasconcelos has labeled a "cosmic race."

During the next three centuries under Spanish rule, Mexican culture emerged as an amalgamation of its diverse roots. Not only did indigenous peoples, Spaniards, and their mixed progeny contribute to this unique blend, but the arrival of approximately a quarter million African slaves between 1519 and 1700 added to the mixture. Even as cultures clashed and blended, their roots—indigenous, Spanish, and African—have never disappeared completely in Mexico.

THE COMPONENTS OF THE COSMIC RACE

Indigenous people have lived in what is now Mexico for many thousands of years. The ancestors of the Aztecs and Maya migrated from Southeast Asia to North America via a land connection at the present location of the Bering Straits and rapidly spread south throughout the double continent. Mesoamerica—the area including contemporary Mexico and Central America—soon emerged as one of the most densely populated regions in the Americas, and around 2000 BCE,* its inhabitants began to build cities. The first indigenous civilization that left behind extensive archaeological evidence was that of the Olmecs, who lived in the tropical lowlands in present-day Veracruz and Tabasco. Giant stone heads and other artifacts there date from around 1200 BCE.

Almost a millennium later, three major clusters of indigenous civilizations emerged: Teotihuacán in the valley of Mexico, or Anáhuac; Monte Albán, Oaxaca; and the Maya city-states in the Yucatán peninsula and Central America. In what is known as the classic period (200 BCE–900 CE), these civilizations founded great cities that were not only centers of worship, but also commercial hubs and places of residence for a socially differentiated population. Many of the structures in these cities have survived to the present day, displaying the notable architectural and artistic achievements of the classic period. By 500 CE, Teotihuacán had at least 100,000 inhabitants, more than any European city of the time, and its imposing Sun Pyramid remains the highest such structure outside Egypt. Led by a king and a theocratic elite of priests, the people worshipped a complex pantheon of gods, chief among them Quetzalcóatl, the plumed serpent.

Centered on city-states such as Palenque, Tikal, and Uxmal, the Maya world developed a bit later than Teotihuacán, around 300 CE. Dependent on seasonal rainfall, the Mayas developed such sophisticated mathematical and dating systems that their calendar—a combination of solar and lunar years—is

* before the common era

off by less than a minute after thousands of years. As in Teotihuacán, natural phenomena corresponded to representative gods in a polytheistic religion as characterized by gods and goddesses of the sun, rain, and fertility, among others. The gods' ties to nature signified the deep connection between the Maya and their environment. For example, when there was either too much or too little rain, the Maya practiced rituals to appease their gods. These rituals often involved the shedding of human or animal blood, as indigenous peoples throughout Mesoamerica believed that blood was life. Land belonged to the community, a community dominated by a king and a caste of priests who monopolized knowledge, power, and religious authority. The Maya caste system left an individual's station in society fixed—with few exceptions—and in some Maya city states, members of the upper castes even deformed the heads of babies in order to create visibly apparent physical distinctions.

With good reason, a novel by the Guatemalan writer Miguel Angel Asturias labels the indigenous people of Mesoamerica as *hombres de maíz*, or people of corn. Indeed, the indigenous worldview revolved around the cultivation of maize, usually in a *milpa*, or raised field, together with beans and squash. A Maya myth, the *Popol Vuh*, told the human creation story as successive attempts by three water-dwelling plumed serpents. First, they attempted to make mud into humans, but their creations could neither move nor speak. Next, they made a set out of wood, but the new humans had neither a soul nor blood. Finally, the serpents decided to make humans out of maize, resulting in the creation of the Maya. The Popol Vuh reflects the great attachment of Mesoamerican peoples to the cultivation of corn. Yet the artistic and scientific accomplishments of the postclassic civilizations should not suggest that they were peaceful societies devoted to agriculture and the study of nature and the universe. Instead, these societies were often at war with their neighbors, and recent research demonstrates that both Teotihuacán and the Maya states practiced human sacrifice for god-appeasement and celebrations.

Around 900 CE, migrations reshaped the indigenous world and ushered in the postclassic period (900–1519 CE). The primary reasons for these migrations were climate change and economic degradation as a result of land cultivation. This post-classic period was marked by the formation of large empires, especially in present-day central Mexico, and more intense and technologically advanced forms of warfare in the Maya region. At the beginning of this period, the Toltecs, a warlike, nomadic people, established their capital at Tula in what is now the state of Hidalgo, where tall stone figures still bear witness to their mark on the region. The Toltecs followed religious practices that pitted a militaristic god, Tezcatlipoca (or Smoking Mirror), against Topiltzín-Quetzalcóatl, a newer, benevolent version of the Teotihuacán deity.

Pointing to apparent similarities between Quetzalcóatl and Kukulcán, a Maya god, archaeologists and historians long believed that the Toltecs also overran the Maya city-states in the Yucatán. The resultant cultural fusion, these scholars argued, produced new architecture such as the northern half of Chichén Itzá, including the famous Temple of the Sorcerer. Recent research suggests, however, that the Toltec conquest of Yucatán never occurred. Instead, scholars point to the Putún Maya, a civilization located in present-day Tabasco, or between the Toltecs and Yucatec Maya, as cultural mediators between central Mexico and Yucatán. In any event, Chichén Itzá became the most powerful city in Yucatán, and perhaps the largest urban settlement in eleventh-century Mesoamerica. For reasons that remain debated, most of its inhabitants abandoned Chichén Itzá after 1100 CE, possibly as a consequence of crop failure or another natural catastrophe.

Even as the Toltecs and Itzá consolidated their rule, another warlike people came from the north, from a legendary place they called Aztlán (most likely present-day Oklahoma or Texas). The Aztecs numbered among the Chichimeca, an assortment of nomadic communities that entered the Valley of Mexico in the eleventh century CE. The Aztecs initially settled eighteen miles southwest of the former Teotihuacán, near Chapultepec Hill, but remained nomadic. Legend has it that they left Aztlán upon the command of their primary god, Huitzilopochtli, or hummingbird, who instructed them to perform human sacrifice in his name. Throughout the Valley of Mexico—and particularly around Lake Texcoco—the Aztecs were reviled for their cruelty; for that reason, local towns hired them as mercenaries. Finally, beginning in 1325, the Aztecs built a city on an island in the middle of the lake. According to legend, an Aztec leader named Tenoch decided on the site after seeing an eagle perched on a nopal cactus with a serpent in its beak—much later, the Mexican coat of arms. This city became known as Tenochtitlán.

In the fifteenth century, Tenochtitlán emerged as the largest city in the Western Hemisphere. Its growth rested on revolutionary agricultural techniques that included the use of *chinampas*, or floating gardens, to allow year-long cultivation of crops. The aqueducts and drainage systems needed to support these techniques as well as a growing population represented an unprecedented achievement in engineering. By 1500, the population of Tenochtitlán approached 200,000 inhabitants. The Aztec capital was an architectural marvel. As the Spanish conquistador Bernal Díaz del Castillo wrote: "We were astounded when we saw all those cities and villages built in the water ... these great towns, temples, and buildings, all made of stone and rising from the water, seemed like an enchanted vision." Indeed, the lake was crucial to the rise of Tenochtitlán. The Aztecs used the lake around them not just as a

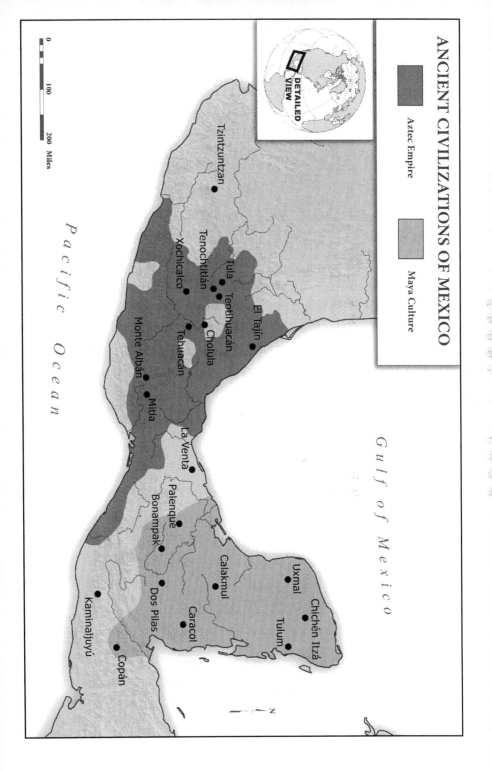

source of irrigation, but also as a highway for their canoes, through which they obtained invaluable commercial advantages over their neighbors.

By the time Díaz and other Spaniards arrived in Mesoamerica, Tenochtitlán had become the center of a vast empire. Superior to their neighbors in technological and military terms, the Aztecs subjugated the peoples of central and southern Mexico by means of a tribute system that collected from villages as far away as the Gulf of Mexico and the Pacific Ocean. By 1500, the Aztecs claimed dominion over an estimated 15 to 25 million people. Tribute collection depended on clientelist arrangements with local leaders, or *caciques*, and it involved the provision of food, pottery, handwoven items, and forced labor, among other goods and services. In return, the Aztecs supported the caciques against their adversaries. The Aztec Empire entered the period of its greatest glory under the reign of Moctezuma II, who came to power in 1502.

However, Moctezuma's rule also manifested widespread discontent with the Aztec dominion. The Aztecs subscribed to a brutal religion that demanded ever-increasing human sacrifice. They believed that they lived in the era of the "fifth sun," a period in which human sacrifice was required in order to keep the sun shining. The Aztec nobility thus took the ancient belief that blood equaled life to its extreme. They promoted the idea that the chief god Quetzalcóatl had fled from Mesoamerica in a state of intoxication, leaving the bloodthirsty god Huitzilopochtli to dominate the region. The emperor considered himself the representative of Huitzilopochtli. During his reign, the imposing temples of Tenochtitlán—and particularly what we now know as the Templo Mayor, the high temple of the emperor—featured awesome displays of power, including the ritual sacrifice of captured enemy soldiers, chiefly among them the Tlaxcaltecos, members of a civilization sixty miles to the east that had not submitted to Aztec rule. Aztec priests cut out the hearts of the victims with obsidian blades, offering them to Huitzilopochtli as his blood sacrifice so that the empire might continue to prosper. The mounting human toll was but one sign that the realm of Moctezuma was in deep distress at the moment of its greatest power. A small class of Aztec priest-rulers, the *pipiltín*, lorded over a vast majority of commoners and serfs, and they had cast aside the communal landholding patterns of the past to emerge as a landowning aristocracy. Across the far-flung empire, local communities merely tolerated the Aztec military presence, hoping for a chance to break free in the near future.

Farther to the east, the Maya world underwent a different kind of transformation. For reasons that remain the subject of intense debate among archaeologists and historians, the Maya had abandoned most of their great cities during the preceding centuries. Some scholars have blamed overcultivation and crop failure, which might have induced the city dwellers to disperse. Others point to the practice of ritual bloodletting among the elite, which often took the form of self-mutilation, as evidence that Maya states were experiencing a crisis of leadership. Yet others hypothesize that the Maya interpreted a single natural disaster, such as an earthquake or the strike of a large meteorite, as a sign of the impending end of their world. In any event, by the time a Spanish expedition reached Yucatán in 1517, the Maya age of glory had long passed.

Although they had never met the Aztecs or Maya up to the day they reached Yucatán, the Spaniards shared several important cultural traits with the indigenous people they were about to conquer. Like the Aztec Empire, sixteenth-century Spain was a monarchy featuring a landowning aristocracy and a close association between the state and organized militaristic religion. And both the Aztecs and the Maya could relate to one of the central tenets of Christianity—the idea that salvation came to the faithful through Jesus's sacrifice and the shedding of his blood on the cross. Modern Spain emerged in the late 1400s out of the union of the two largest Iberian kingdoms by the marriage of Ferdinand of Aragón and Isabella of Castile. Located in the extreme southwest of Europe and separated from Africa only by the forty-mile Straits of Gibraltar, the Iberian Peninsula was a major meeting point of peoples: the indigenous Iberians and Basques, the Phoenicians, Greeks, and Romans of the ancient Mediterranean, Jewish refugees, the Visigoths, and the Moors, Muslims of Arabic extraction.

Of these peoples, the Romans and Moors left the most lasting impact on the region. Its inhabitants would go on to establish vast colonial empires stretching from the Philippines to California to Tierra del Fuego. Rome dominated Iberia for seven hundred years (c. 216 BCE–476 CE), and a variant of Latin, enriched by Iberian, Basque, and Arabic words, evolved into the Spanish and Portuguese languages of today. The imperial Roman political system—a fusion of authoritarian rule, bureaucratic administration, and the trappings of parliamentary decisionmaking—imprinted itself on Iberia. Roman law survives in the legal codes of Spain and Portugal as well as their former colonies, and both Judaism and Christianity came to Iberia through the trade routes of the Roman Empire. The Moors invaded Iberia in 711 CE and destroyed the Visigoth kingdom that featured a small Germanic ruling class governing a multiethnic society. The Moors established their rule over more than 90 percent of the Iberian Peninsula and founded one of the greatest cities of the Muslim world, Córdoba, in the southern province they called Al-Andalus, contemporary Andalusia. Under Muslim rule, Iberia flourished economically and culturally, and the Qur'an's toleration of Judaism and Christianity produced a unique society. The ruling class was Muslim, as only Muslims were allowed to bear arms; most of the peasants were Christian; and a significant percentage of the urban professionals were Jewish. But this civilization was never at peace. At first, the Muslims pushed on into what is now France, only to be repelled, then several small Christian kingdoms in the unconquered north of Iberia began their own offensive against the Moors.

Thus began what subsequent Spanish historiography would label the *reconquista*, or age of reconquest. In the course of the next four centuries, the Christian kingdoms pushed south against their Muslim enemies, promising land and booty to those who led their troops into battle. The reconquista produced a crusading and wealthy Church bent on expanding its influence as well as a powerful feudal nobility conscious of its role. This nobility ruled over its conquered subjects—whether Christian, Jewish, or Muslim—with an iron fist. By the twelfth century, the reconquista slowed, and Aragón, Castile, and Portugal had emerged as the primary Christian kingdoms, with Al-Andalus remaining a Muslim monarchy until after Ferdinand and Isabella's marriage in 1469 aligned Aragón and Castile. The slowing of the reconquista meant fewer opportunities for the warring nobles who had benefited from the expansion of Christian lands at the expense of the Muslims. Moreover, the principle of primogeniture restricted land inheritance to the eldest son, leaving the younger sons to pursue careers in the Church, the bureaucracy, or the military. The Spaniards called these dispossessed aristocrats *hidalgos*, a term that derived from the phrase *hijo de algo*, or son of something. Determined to destroy the remaining Muslim kingdom, Isabella persuaded Ferdinand to join Castile in an attack on Al-Andalus. In 1492, the combined troops of Aragón and Castile conquered Andalusia. But Isabella, who later received the byname *la católica*, the Catholic Queen, was not done in her quest to "purify" her kingdom of its enemies. That same year, she and Ferdinand expelled all Jewish inhabitants from their combined kingdom.

If 1492 marked the end of the reconquista, it also signified the beginning of a new age of conquest: a new opportunity for the hidalgos and others in search of social and political advancement. On October 12 of that same year, Columbus's expedition stumbled upon the New World while looking for a sea route to India—a route that the Portuguese, Iberian rivals of the Spaniards, had been seeking for almost a century in their explorations around the coast of Africa. This expedition was therefore part of an age in which Spain and Portugal took the enterprise of conquest overseas. The conquistadors engaged in this endeavor sought "God, gold, and glory," i.e., the spread of Christianity, personal enrichment, and political power. Indeed, they did so with the

Church's blessing. In 1493, Isabella and Ferdinand struck an unprecedented deal with Pope Alexander VI—the so-called *patronato real*, or kingly patronage—that assured them of the Vatican's support in their enterprise of conquest in exchange for their pledge to defend Catholicism across the globe. In a papal bull, Alexander awarded Spain all newly explored lands to the west of a north-south meridian 100 miles west of the Cape Verde Islands. Of course, in drawing this line, he never asked the opinion of any of the inhabitants of the affected territories. This line would have opened up all of the Americas to Spanish colonization if the subsequent Treaty of Tordesillas, signed in 1494, had not moved the line 1,000 miles west. The Tordesillas treaty opened eastern South America to Portuguese colonization. The alliance between Pope Alexander and the Spanish monarchs was but one important aspect of a special relationship. The late fifteenth century witnessed the establishment of the Spanish Inquisition, an ecclesiastical high court charged with purging the realm of witches, infidels, and half-hearted converts to Christianity. This court gained sweeping powers to investigate Spanish subjects, and conviction often meant death.

When Columbus and other explorers returned from the New World with tales of unknown riches, many hidalgos jumped at the chance to participate in new military conquests. They saw the conquest of the New World as an opportunity to reclaim the social status of their forebears. Steeled by centuries of conflict and repression in the reconquista, the hidalgos were well suited to confront civilizations culturally different from their own. By the time Isabella and Ferdinand's grandson, Charles I of Habsburg, became king of Spain in 1516, hidalgos had featured prominently in the conquest of Cuba and the other Caribbean islands.

In 1519, it was one of these hidalgos, Hernán (or Fernando) Cortés who took the command of an expedition to explore the vast territories to the southwest of Cuba. Cortés was a native of the province of Extremadura in western Spain, an arid region with few opportunities even for the fortunate. He hailed from a noble family of modest means that desired him to pursue a career in law—along with the army and the Church, one of the hidalgos' career avenues for social climbing. Yet young Hernán, born only seven years before Columbus's first voyage to America, dreamed of participating in the Spanish conquest of the West Indies. In 1504, he boarded a ship to the New World, and seven years later, he formed part of the Spanish army that conquered the island of Cuba. Once there, Cortés took a position in the colonial government and became a man of considerable prosperity. In this capacity, he knew of two Spanish expeditions to a vast land southwest of Cuba. In 1517, an expedition under Francisco Hernández de Córdoba reached the coast of Yucatán, a peninsula then believed to be an island; and the following year, Juan de Grijalva's expedition visited what is now the Gulf Coast of Mexico and brought home several small gold objects. Grijalva and his charges told stories of a legendary land of gold that, they believed, lay in the heart of the area they were about to encounter. Intrigued, Cortés hired many of the men who had participated in these earlier forays for his own attempt to conquer the lands to the west. On February 18, 1519, Cortés and a small force of approximately 550 set out for Yucatán.

Contrary to a stereotype passed down by generations of historians, this expedition was not primarily composed of hidalgos or other noblemen. Poor nobles comprised a small minority among Cortés's troops, which included men from all social strata such as sailors, artisans, and craftsmen, as well as a handful of women. Regardless of their standing in society, the conquistadors sought power and wealth they could only obtain through an opportunity such as this one. Nor was the expedition an exclusively Spanish enterprise. Cortés's force comprised people from Portugal, Germany, and Italy, for example.

THE SPANISH CONQUEST AND ITS AFTERMATH, 1519–c. 1630

The stuff of legends and epic tales, the Spanish conquest of the Aztec Empire has generated a great many misconceptions. The intriguing question of how a small invasion force could overpower an empire of millions of subjects has triggered a host of explanations, often founded on myth. For instance, many textbooks still claim that Moctezuma initially welcomed the Spaniards rather than killing them because he and his advisers believed that Cortés was the exiled Quetzalcóatl returning to reclaim his rightful throne from the usurper Huitzilopochtli. According to this tale, Malintzín, an indigenous woman and an aide and translator to Cortés, informed the Spaniards of the Quetzalcóatl myth and thus assisted them in a game of deception that allowed the Spaniards to sneak into the heart of the Aztec Empire. Invented by Bernardino de Sahagún, a sixteenth-century Spanish friar and chronicler of Aztec oral histories of the conquest, this entertaining story makes for powerful human drama, highlights Spanish resourcefulness, and turns Malintzín into a Mexican Mata Hari, whose betrayal of her people led to the fall of the empire. The myth, however, obscures the true reasons for the Spanish triumph: their technological superiority, the introduction of diseases hitherto unknown in Mesoamerica, and—most important—the role played by indigenous enemies of the Aztecs.

Luck, the element of surprise, and superior weaponry helped the Spaniards in the first weeks of their expedition, adding to Cortés's considerable skill as a military commander. During his first stop on the island of Cozumel off the coast of the Yucatán, Cortés encountered Jerónimo de Aguilar, a Franciscan friar who had been shipwrecked eight years before on his way from Panama to Santo Domingo and had attained fluency in the local Mayan dialect. During a subsequent stop on the coast of present-day Tabasco, Cortés obtained twenty slave women, among them Malintzín, who spoke both Mayan and Náhuatl. Together, Aguilar and Malintzín gave Cortés the ability to communicate with the Aztecs. Soon after landing on the Gulf Coast and founding Veracruz, the first Spanish settlement in Mesoamerica, Cortés and his men turned inland. At Cempoala, the Spaniards defeated a smaller indigenous army. This confrontation pitted indigenous troops on foot, armed with stone weapons against armored soldiers on horseback. The Spaniards' single greatest technological advantage was their use of metal and gunpowder. Their guns could kill scores of indigenous troops from a distance, and the invaders' swords were vastly more effective than the obsidian blades and spear tips used by the indigenous armies. In addition, the horse—an animal bred exclusively in the Old World at that time—gave the Spaniards great advantages over their indigenous adversaries. It is also worth noting that the Spaniards possessed distinctive strategic advantages in their style of warfare; while the Aztecs' priority lay in the capture of prisoners for use in ceremonies of human sacrifice, the Spaniards focused on defeating and killing their enemies.

Once other indigenous communities realized that they could not stop the Spanish invasion force, many of them decided to support Cortés in the hopes of throwing off the yoke of the Aztec Empire, who under Moctezuma, had greatly increased imperial demands for tribute from subject peoples. Cortés's powerful indigenous allies were the most important factor in his eventual victory; so much so that the conquest was a joint venture, an "Indian conquest" as much as a "Spanish conquest." Moctezuma had one inveterate opponent in Xicoténcatl the Elder, the ruler of Tlaxcala. Xicoténcatl and other leading Tlaxcaltecos resented the Aztec ruler's ritualistic sacrifices of their warriors on the Templo Mayor, and they longed for a chance to destroy his empire. After his troops had lost a skirmish with Cortés's force, Xicoténcatl decided to assist the Spaniards.

From Tlaxcala, Cortés and his troops proceeded to the city of Cholula, a mere sixty miles east of Tenochtitlán. Once allied with Xicoténcatl, the city had recently joined the Aztecs. Warned by Malintzín, who by then had learned to communicate in Spanish, Cortés suspected a trap at Cholula and ordered his troops to fire on the local leadership, which had assembled to greet him upon his entrance to the city. During the ensuing fight, as many as 6,000 Cholulans lost their lives. Frightened by the Spaniards' display of deadly violence and uncertain whether their coming represented divine intervention, Moctezuma agreed to meet with Cortés on the causeway leading to Tenochtitlán. During this meeting on November 8, 1519, Malintzín again played an important role. As she had done in the Spanish negotiations with other indigenous leaders, she provided Cortés with important information regarding local society and culture. It even appears that she took on authority of her own, as Cortés trusted and valued her judgment on the indigenous people with whom he was dealing. Confident of success, Cortés bluntly informed Moctezuma that he and his companions suffered from a "disease of the heart that [could] only be cured with gold." This statement demonstrated the Spaniards' greed, implying that Cortés and his men certainly fought for gold and glory as well as for the proclaimed purpose of extending the global reach of Christianity. Uncertain of what to do, Moctezuma ordered gold jewelry delivered and invited the Spaniards into Tenochtitlán. But the Spanish conquistador suspected another trap, and once in the Aztec capital, Cortés decided to deal a preemptive strike by taking Moctezuma hostage.

This scheme might have delayed hostilities for quite a while had Cortés not received word of the coming of a rival, Pánfilo Narváez, the leader of another Spanish expedition. To confront Narváez, Cortés returned to Cempoala, leaving a detachment of troops in the Aztec capital under the leadership of Pedro de Alvarado. Cortés handily defeated the Narváez expedition and augmented his own troops with hundreds of Narváez's men. In Cortés's absence, the Aztecs staged a ceremony to honor Huitzilopochtli—a feast designed to show that their institutions and rituals continued to function even with the Spaniards in their city. The inexperienced Alvarado was nervous about what he considered a threat to the Spanish garrison and ordered his troops to attack the Aztec aristocracy during the ceremony. The attack was brutal and bloody; in the words of the Spanish chronicler Bernardino de Sahagún, "the blood of the chiefs ran like water." It also marked the beginning of open hostilities, and the Aztecs elected a new leader, Cuitláhuac, in place of the captive Moctezuma. At this juncture, Cortés and his men reentered the city, and the conquistador persuaded Moctezuma to ask his people to allow the Spaniards to leave peacefully. Even before Moctezuma had finished speaking, however, the Aztecs pelted him with rocks, and the former emperor died in the ensuing melee. We still do not know the exact circumstances of his death: while Bernal Díaz claimed that Moctezuma died as a result of the stoning, indigenous accounts indicated that the Spaniards killed him. Whatever the case may be, Cortés knew that the Spaniards could not stay in the Aztec capital any longer and ordered a daring departure from Tenochtitlán across the narrow causeways that connected the city to the edge of the lake. On July 1, 1520, in what became known in Conquest lore as *la noche triste*, or the sad night, the Spaniards attempted their escape from the island city. Loaded down with gold and other booty, at least 450 Spaniards died during the escape.

The Spanish exodus allowed Cortés to plan a full assault on the Aztec Empire. With the help of tens of thousands of Tlaxcalteco troops, Cortés laid siege to Tenochtitlán. In 1521, the allies took Tenochtitlán and captured the last Aztec emperor, Cuauhtémoc. To demonstrate their power, the Spaniards razed the Aztec city and built a new capital, the Ciudad de México (Mexico City) over the ruins of its temples. Dragged from his homeland to accompany the Spaniards in the conquest of southeastern Mesoamerica, Cuauhtémoc died in captivity.

As mentioned, the inadvertent introduction of Old World diseases played an important role in the Aztec defeat. Smallpox, measles, and other viral diseases appeared in Mesoamerica in the wake of Narváez's expedition, spreading quickly. While Europeans and Africans had acquired significant immunity against these diseases in the course of several millennia of exposure, the immune systems of indigenous Americans had little defense against the new germs. Even before the Spaniards and Tlaxcaltecos overpowered Tenochtitlán, the mysterious deaths of thousands of indigenous people had weakened Aztec resolve. These deaths were particularly important in a society dominated by a belief system that emphasized its ties to nature and the need to appease the gods in charge of natural forces. In the long term, the consequences were even more devastating. Over the next century, the native population fell to approximately 1 million, a decline of at least 92 percent.

This population decline determined the characteristics of Spanish rule, and, in particular, the systems of forced labor imposed by the conquerors. The deaths of millions of indigenous peoples undercut efforts by the conquistadors to make themselves into a noble class in what was now the colony of New Spain. The conquistadors expected to be handsomely rewarded by Spain for their exploits, and Cortés himself attained a new noble title: the Marquis of the Valley of Oaxaca. As the Spaniards never found the gold they were looking for when they sought the mythical El Dorado, these rewards came in the form of the labor grant, or *encomienda*. A grant of encomienda entitled a conquistador to dominion over the indigenous community or communities listed in the title in exchange for the theoretical commitment to bring Christianity to the indigenous people. In practice, the encomienda became a tribute system in which *caciques* (local chiefs) could either pay or provide indigenous labor. Thus the conquistadors used the encomienda both as an instrument of tribute and as a justification for keeping thousands of indigenous people in conditions of forced labor even as many of these people were permitted to keep their lands and other property. Over time, the decline of the indigenous population rendered most of the caciques unable to meet their obligations to the *encomenderos*. At the very time when the native nobility was disappearing, the encomienda system came under attack in Spain, as the Crown feared that the encomiendas would evolve into hereditary feudal fiefdoms that it could not control. Desiring to impose his authority on the conquistadors and their descendants, Charles I issued the New Laws of 1542, which promised to end the encomienda and outlawed the enslavement of indigenous Americans on the grounds that they—unlike the Africans—had not yet had the opportunity to embrace Jesus Christ as their savior. In response, the conquistadors moved to assume more direct control over native land and labor. By 1600, two new institutions had begun to replace the encomienda: the *repartimiento*, which required indigenous communities to contribute a percentage of laborers to nearby Spanish authorities, and the hacienda, the great agricultural estate held in private hands.

The controversy regarding the exploitation of indigenous labor highlighted the tensions between the Crown and its subjects in New Spain; tensions that demonstrated the chasm between the theory and practice of the colonial government. The official representative of the Spanish king was the viceroy in Mexico City, a native Spaniard appointed to a six-year term. To provide a system of checks and balances in government, the king also appointed a legislative and judicial body, the *audiencia*. At the regional level, *corregidores* and *alcaldes mayores* answered to the viceroy. In practice, however, the viceroy depended to a great extent on the goodwill of the conquistador families. Thus the encomienda survived for centuries in spite of the New Laws, and local authorities often ignored directives from Mexico City.

Rather than the colonial government, however, it was the Church that was the most important institution in the making of colonial New Spain. The Church was responsible for molding the hearts and minds of the conquered peoples according to the cultural values of the conquistadors, and it played a significant role in the cultural transformation that occurred in colonial New Spain. Under the patronato real, the Crown had pledged itself to convert all indigenous peoples to Christianity, and the Spanish monarchs considered the defense and advancement of the Catholic Church one of their most important missions. This endeavor became even more important during the Protestant Reformation in Europe, which coincided with the era of the Iberian conquest of the New World. Thus Franciscan friars had accompanied Cortés's expedition to Mesoamerica. Unlike conquistadors, Franciscan and Dominican friars vowed to lead a life of chastity, poverty, and obedience, and they stood at the forefront of the conversion effort.

Yet conversion of indigenous peoples to Catholicism proved to be a complex undertaking. In the first place, the friars were greatly outnumbered in comparison to the native population. The friars soon found out that they needed to accept indigenous idols and beliefs in order to succeed in their efforts at conversion, thus creating syncretic religious practices that blended Catholic and indigenous ideas. The foremost example of such a syncretism is the cult of Our Lady of Guadalupe, the "patron" saint of Mexico who reputedly appeared to an indigenous campesino, Juan Diego Cuauhtlatoatzín, on December 9, 1531. According to historians, this cult either represents a convergence of the Catholic Virgin Mary and the Aztec goddess Tonantzín, or it is a Catholic rendition of Coatlicue, the Aztec goddess and mother of Huitzilopochtli. As the story goes, Juan Diego saw Guadalupe as the Virgin Mary, speaking to him in Náhuatl. Guadalupe asked Juan Diego to tell the bishop to build a shrine at the site of the encounter, Tepeyac Hill just north of the new capital city, so that she might bestow her grace on all those who sought her. Skeptical of Juan Diego's vision, the local bishop requested evidence that the apparition was true. But on December 12, the Virgin ordered Juan Diego to return to Tepeyac. That day, Juan Diego found a rose bush flowering in the midst of winter and took some of the flowers to the bishop. When the roses fell from his mantle, the image of the Virgin was imprinted on the cloth. Satisfied with the legitimacy of Juan Diego's vision, the bishop ordered the erection of a shrine to Guadalupe at Tepeyac. Since then, December 12 has been celebrated as the *día de Guadalupe* throughout Mexico and its diaspora. A fusion of indigenous and Spanish cultural traditions, the cult of Guadalupe remains an essential element in the Mexican national consciousness. In the words of novelist Carlos Fuentes, "One may no longer consider himself a Christian, but one cannot truly be considered a Mexican unless one believes in the Virgin of Guadalupe."

The story of the Virgin of Guadalupe stood in contrast to the "Black Legend" of Malintzín. The help that this indigenous woman provided to the Spaniards—and the fact that she probably gave birth to the first mestizo, Martín Cortés, following an amorous relationship with the leader of the conquistadors—earned her widespread condemnation. In fact, even today,

Malintzín, or La Malinche, stands for treasonous behavior, and *malinchismo* is a noun that denotes a Mexican who has either turned his or her back on the fatherland or is actively betraying Mexican interests. While the Spaniards admiringly referred to Malintzín as "doña Marina," many Mexicans called her *la chingada*, a term that means "whore," or someone who has been sexually violated. Paired with Guadalupe, Malintzín therefore represents one of the sides in the madonna/whore dichotomy used in many Catholic societies to classify women according to a presumed sexual propriety or impropriety. In fact, a closer look paints a more sympathetic picture of Malintzín. A noble woman who had been sold into slavery by allies of the Aztecs, she did not owe the Aztecs any allegiance, and she may have seen herself as only one of the millions of indigenous people who helped the Spaniards throw off the yoke of a hated empire. If we accept the notion of the "Indian conquest," that is to say, an interpretation that focuses on the contribution of indigenous opponents of Moctezuma in the destruction of Tenochtitlán, Malintzín played a rather typical, if prominent role in advancing the agenda of the enemies of the Aztecs. Just like Xicoténcatl and the other Spanish allies, she could not possibly have fathomed that the arrival of several hundred outsiders would signal the end of the indigenous world as she knew it. Male-dominated post-conquest lore did not castigate the Tlaxcalans to nearly the same extent as Malintzín, even though Xicoténcatl and his men had played a significant role in the triumph of the Spaniards.

Far from being mere instruments of conquest, the friars living among the indigenous people sometimes turned into staunch advocates for them. The famous Franciscan friar and former encomendero Bartolomé de las Casas assailed the conquistadors—and particularly the encomienda—for its cruelty to native peoples. Las Casas's treatise *The Devastation of the Indies* still stands as the most eloquent denunciation of the atrocities of Spanish colonialism. Las Casas's ideas were to play a significant role in the formulation of the New Laws, which forbade the formal enslavement of indigenous peoples. Another friar, Toribio de Benavente, or Motolinía, was known as the "Poor Little One" in reference to his modest appearance and advocacy for the poor. Other churchmen such as Bernardino de Sahagún and the first bishop of Yucatán, Diego de Landa, were fascinated with indigenous cultures and saw it as their obligation to record the oral and written histories of the Aztecs and Maya. Ironically, after writing what remains the most important conquest-era description of Maya culture, de Landa ordered the destruction of all Maya icons and artifacts that he could find because they were not compatible with Christianity.

The relationship between royal officials and the Church was another example of the differences between policy and practice. Under the patronato real, the state pledged itself to supporting the Christianization of the indigenous people in the colony, while the Pope promised to stay out of political affairs and even allowed the Crown to name the archbishop in Mexico City as well as other top clergy. As a result, the higher rungs of the Catholic hierarchy in New Spain—archbishops and bishops—worked closely with the colonial government. For example, in 1571, the Crown and Church cooperated in installing the Inquisition in New Spain, and over the next quarter millennium, the Inquisition brought approximately 6,000 individuals to trial, with 100 defendants burned at the stake for heresy. In practice, however, this partnership did not always work well. The viceroy permitted abuses against the native population to continue unabated, and the lower clergy often clashed with Spanish mine and landowners over their harsh treatment of their workers. There was little communication between the Church hierarchy in the cities and the missionaries in the countryside. One particular religious order that came to Mexico in the late sixteenth century, the Jesuits, ignored the arrangement between Church and state altogether, built their missions far away from Spanish-dominated cities, and defied the authority of the Crown.

By about 1600, the indigenous population had stabilized, Catholicism was entrenched, and a new society had emerged. In theory, the colony was divided into "castes," based on a person's ethnic or racial origin. Thus Spanish colonial law recognized more than sixty racial classifications ranging from a pure-blooded Spaniard to the product of an African-indigenous union. Social status loosely corresponded to one's degree of "whiteness," and relatively speaking, the caste system stigmatized African origin more so than indigenous heritage. In practice, however, these classifications were not universally recognized. A majority of the inhabitants of New Spain were mestizos, descendants of mixed unions of Spanish men and indigenous and/or African women. About 15 percent of the population was Spanish, with a significant and growing percentage of *creoles* (Mexican-born whites), who felt less attachment to colonial dictates than the native-born Spaniards, also known as *peninsulares*. Another 20 percent was indigenous, defined as people who continued to speak indigenous languages and practice the culture of the Aztecs and other native peoples. The remainder was African, both slave and free, a group concentrated along the coasts of central and southern Mexico and in the largest cities.

African slaves and freedmen probably first entered Mexico as part of the ill-fated Narváez expedition. These African slaves formed part of a story often forgotten amidst the epic clash of civilizations in the conquest of Mexico. Indeed, the institution of slavery, and the forced migration of Africans that it produced, was an integral part of the enterprise of conquest. By the time Cortés embarked on his adventure, thousands of African slaves worked on sugar plantations as well as in private households and many other locations in Cuba, the other Caribbean islands, and on the Iberian peninsula itself. Accustomed to tropical climates and largely immune to Old World pathogens, the slaves survived conditions that had proven fatal for the indigenous people.

Africans and their descendants constituted an important element of the colonial crucible. During the sixteenth and seventeenth centuries, more than 200,000 slaves (the equivalent of 10 percent of the transatlantic slave trade) arrived in Mexico. To be sure, African slaves never accounted for more than 2 percent of the population, and they did not suffer the impact of the people in areas where Old World diseases virtually wiped out the indigenous population, as in Cuba, the Portuguese colony of Brazil, or in British possessions such as Jamaica or South Carolina. Nonetheless, Afro-Mexicans left indelible traces on the evolving culture. They worked on plantations, in mines, in textile sweatshops, and as domestics. Working under brutal conditions, Africans created social networks that allowed them to retain some aspects of their cultural heritage. To this day, the regional cultures of the coastal states of Guerrero, Oaxaca, and Veracruz—particularly with regard to music, dance, and food—remain influenced by their African roots. Social networks also allowed slaves to rebel against their conditions, although rebellion came at a heavy price: whipping, mutilation, and even death. Some slaves fled to distant runaway slave communities, or *palenques*. Yanga, the leader of the most famous palenque in the mountains of Veracruz, forced the authorities to recognize the independence of his town, and he remains a symbol of black resistance even today. Ultimately, however, the Afro-Mexican population became absorbed in the miscegenated population.

Although Spanish colonial legislation carefully distinguished among Spaniards, "Indians," Africans, and mestizos, even subdividing the latter into sixteen categories based on their racial ancestry, the reality was more fluid. In rare cases, prosperous nonwhites could purchase a certificate—the *gracias al sacar*—that certified the holder to be a Christian of pure Spanish descent. This example demonstrated the primacy of class over racial categories even though social stratification roughly followed color lines. Indigenous people who spoke Spanish also could blend into mestizo society when they so desired. Further differentiated at the regional and local levels, colonial Mexican society presaged the patchwork of regional and social identities that would characterize the mature colony and beyond. Equally fluid as the caste system was the court system of the viceroyalty. In theory, a system of *fueros*, laws bestowing special privileges, established separate areas of jurisdiction for the army, the Church, and the indigenous population, respectively. In practice, however, the legal system became an area in which indigenous people and mestizos contested and resisted colonial rule, and recent scholarship has demonstrated the many ways in which poor Mexicans—particularly those of indigenous and African descent—used the courts to their own advantage.

The ongoing cultural clashes highlighted the fact that the Spanish conquest had opened Mesoamerica to a relationship with the outside world. Not only had the Spanish conquest changed Mesoamerica, but the region also changed the rest of the world. The "Columbian Exchange" that brought guns and germs to the Americas introduced the Old World to countless products native to present-day Mexico, including maize and the cocoa bean, which had once served as a form of currency in the Aztec Empire and would now have lasting importance on a global scale.

A COLONY IN TRANSITION, C. 1630–C. 1800

The viceroyalty of New Spain was the crown jewel of the Spanish Empire. Buoyed by the export of silver and other commodities, Mexico City became the largest city among Spain's colonial possessions, and also one that enjoyed the closest administrative and cultural relationship with the mother country. Whether as priests, merchants, or artisans, Spaniards continued to migrate to the viceroyalty throughout the colonial era. It is not surprising that this close relationship endured into the nineteenth century, marking Mexican history well beyond the colonial years.

Nonetheless, as New Spain entered the seventeenth century, inhabitants of the viceroyalty remained far less obedient to decrees from Madrid than the Crown expected. From the vantage point of the Spanish government, the revenue from Mexico was a source of disappointment. Having hoped to find tons of gold in the Aztec Empire, the conquistadors discovered that the precious metal was almost as scarce in Mesoamerica as it was in Europe. Instead, the Spaniards found silver in the mountains of present-day central Mexico. While the sixteenth century witnessed a steady flow of silver to Spain to help finance a host of imperial wars against Britain, France, and the Ottoman Empire, Mexican silver mining initially remained modest compared to that in Peru. Moreover, the price of silver declined precipitously in the early seventeenth century.

Mexico, however, featured a burgeoning internal economy beginning in the seventeenth century. Rather than investing in silver mining, wealthy creoles turned to manufacturing, and particularly the *obraje*, or textile sweatshop. Supplying the domestic market with relatively inexpensive clothes, the obraje amounted to a first small step toward the growth of manufacturing in the colony. It also provided the first significant source of wage labor for women. Taking advantage of cheap labor in the cities and the virtual absence of competition from abroad, the obraje emerged as the primary producer of garments in New Spain.

It is not surprising that recent scholarship has shattered the old notion of the seventeenth century as a "long siesta" in which Spanish rule continued uncontested in a placid, unchanging colony. Indeed, New Spain was a colony in transition during that century, and in many ways, these decades witnessed the emergence of a complex amalgamation of colonial identities amidst the slow recovery of the indigenous population.

In addition, a series of revolts and riots challenged Spanish rule, demonstrating the strength of local resistance against colonial authorities. Revolts plagued the northern frontier between 1630 and 1750. In this vast and sparsely populated region—an area that spans the entire present-day southwestern United States as well as the northern half of Mexico—indigenous societies continued to operate with minimal Spanish interference and resented Spanish efforts to impose effective control. The nomadic Apaches periodically overran the small Spanish *presidios*, or garrisons, in Sonora, and in 1688, the Pueblo Revolt in New Mexico briefly threw off colonial rule altogether. On the northern frontier, the Jesuit and Franciscan missions were the primary evidence of Spanish colonization. The missionaries built churches that looked like fortresses, with small windows, thick walls, and strong defenses. On the frontier, the Spanish conquest was still taking place centuries after the death of Cortés, and the Yaquis of Sonora were not subdued until the late 1920s.

Closer to their center of power, the Spaniards experienced other problems. Even Mexico City, the epicenter of colonial rule, experienced two great riots in 1624 and 1692. A steep rise in corn prices following failed harvests precipitated both riots, as lower-class Mexicans took to the streets to seek redress for their plight. The *tumulto* of June 8, 1692, in particular, featured mass anger directed at the elite. To the cries of "Death to the *gachupines* (Spaniards)," thousands of mestizos and indigenous Mexicans swept through the capital all the way to the Zócalo, leaving a trail of destruction in their wake. This riot was more than an act of desperation, as the violence reflected an increasing sense of racial identity among mestizos, particularly in urban areas. Royal officials blamed "treacherous Indians" for the looting, but court records show that a majority of the participants convicted for their part in the riot were indigenous and mestizo artisans, shopkeepers, peddlers, and other middling folk.

In addition, the Spaniards could not maintain intellectual and religious conformity in New Spain, particularly in the outer reaches of this far-flung viceroyalty. Despite the presence of the Inquisition, indigenous belief systems remained strong, forcing missionaries and parish priests to be flexible in their interpretation of Christianity centuries after the conquest. As mentioned, the Maya of Chiapas and Yucatán practiced a syncretic religion that blended Christianity with ancient indigenous beliefs; for example, the ancient practice of ritual bloodletting still survives today in the form of the sacrifice of animals. In similar fashion, elements of African belief systems such as African deities and the role of shamans survived in syncretic Afro-Christian practices, particularly in the coastal states of Veracruz, Guerrero, and Oaxaca.

A particularly interesting (though possibly apocryphal) story that highlights the fluidity of identity under Spanish colonial rule is that of Catalina de Erauso, or the "Lieutenant Nun"—a woman who managed to live as a male for many years. Catalina was born into a military family in San Sebastián, Spain, in 1585 and entered a convent at the age of four. Just before taking her vows at the age of fifteen, she gave up life as a nun after a severe beating. Now she disguised herself as a man and embarked for the New World under an assumed name. She enlisted in the Spanish army and fought against the Mapuches in present-day Chile, attaining such military honors that she was promoted to the rank of lieutenant. She became an accomplished warrior and a famed duelist, killing at least a dozen men in duels throughout Spanish America. She fought in present-day Chile, Argentina, and Peru before revealing her gender and returning to Spain. In 1645, however, she went to Veracruz under the name of Antonio de Erauso and continued to live as a man until her death in 1650.

Erauso's successful defiance of the gender norms of her era also mirrors the failure of the Spanish Crown to assert effective control over its colonies. Indeed, the hazards of early modern communications and the arcane political structures of colonial rule gave ample leeway to the king's subjects to ignore or modify his decrees. Long before the arrival of telecommunications, let alone the Internet, the viceroy depended on the Spanish fleet to communicate with his sovereign. Of course, the fleet only sailed back and forth to the Americas once a year. On the regional level, the corregidores enjoyed considerable regional autonomy and only reluctantly responded to the viceroy's initiatives. Finally, vast stretches of New Spain remained frontier, where the indigenous-Spanish encounter continued because the conquistadors lacked the laborers and resources to carry their authority into these distant regions.

Even the elite in the cities eluded the control of the empire. The Spanish ruling class was increasingly marked by a division between the Spanish-born peninsulares and the American-born creoles. The peninsulares occupied most high political and clerical offices, and the posts of viceroy and archbishop were reserved for them. Taking advantage of their immediate family connections with merchants in Seville, natives of Spain dominated overseas commerce.

The creoles owned most privately held land in New Spain, and they occupied most of the positions in the lower bureaucracy and clergy. They also held significant positions in the audiencia in Mexico City, the highest institution in which they could hold office. It appeared to them only a matter of time until they controlled colonial administration. Finally, the creoles could proudly point to significant achievements in architecture, art, music, and literature.

Perhaps no one better epitomized this flowering of creole culture than Sor Juana Inés de la Cruz, probably the greatest Mexican poet and playwright who has ever lived. Born in approximately 1651, Sor Juana grew up within the confines of a liberal convent in Mexico City. A multitalented genius, she stumped a jury of forty university professors who examined her at age seventeen. As was usual at the time, she faced only the choice between marriage (and devoting herself to husband and children) and life as a nun, which offered her somewhat greater freedom in pursuing her literary and scientific interests. Sor Juana chose the latter. At a time when married women did not have access to literacy and books, she was able to amass books and scrolls in her private library within the convent, including many works on the Pope's list of forbidden books. Sor Juana considered her literary work to be part of the tradition of the Spanish Siglo de Oro, or century of gold, but her work transcended these European origins. While closely associated with the viceroy and his wife, she wrote a series of plays that mocked the incompetence of Spanish administrators and the prejudices of the Church. She also wrote early feminist poems that assailed the sexist double standard prevalent in New Spain—a standard that encouraged macho males to seek sexual companionship outside marriage while labeling adulterous females prostitutes. Ultimately, her intellectual ambition led to her downfall after she wrote a treatise criticizing the work of a renowned biblical scholar. This treatise was more than the male hierarchy of Mexico City could take. Pressured by both her abbess and her confessor, Sor Juana recanted and gave away her books, proclaiming herself the "worst of all" women. She ended her life as a devout nun, and became a victim of the plague in 1695.

The increasing confidence of creole society rested on the growing strength of the Mexican economy, particularly in the booming silver-mining sector. Beginning in the late eighteenth century, silver mining in Mexico experienced spectacular growth, while that in Peru declined. And the eighteenth century was Mexico's century of silver, as Spain grew dependent on its colony, rather than the other way around. By 1800, New Spain generated 60 percent of the Crown's colonial revenue. This wealth produced a new social class, the silver kings, powerful enough to purchase noble titles. Even today, names such as the Count of Regla evoke images of limitless personal fortune. Of course, the peons who slaved away in the mines under inhumane conditions paid the price for such wealth. Mine workers seldom lasted more than five years on the job. If the backbreaking labor underground did not kill them, they suffered mercury poisoning, for they used that highly toxic metal to extract silver from the ore. The mine workers, however, were not the only ones whose work amounted to a virtual death sentence. Hundreds of thousands of workers perished in the Huehuetoca, an ambitious (and ultimately only partially successful) effort to drain Lake Texcoco in order to make Mexico City safe from flooding.

At least as far as the silver kings were concerned, the Crown considered their prize colony too prosperous for their own liking. Following the War of the Spanish Succession (1701–13) in Europe, the house of Bourbon had ascended to the throne of Spain. The family that had produced Louis XIV of France, the most powerful king of early modern Europe, viewed Spain as a backward and inefficient kingdom, and they were determined to modernize both the mother country and its colonies. As a result, the Bourbon king Philip V instituted a set of wide-ranging reforms in the colonies, abolishing the trade monopoly of the port city of Cádiz. His successor, Charles III, was determined to bring these reforms to the colonies. In 1765, he sent a visitor general, José de Gálvez, to New Spain on a fact-finding mission. An aristocrat and lawyer, Gálvez spent seven years in the colony, enjoying virtually unlimited powers to examine all aspects of colonial administration. His powers even exceeded those of the viceroy. The visitor general was appalled at what he found. He lambasted a corrupt system in which taxpayers could shirk much of their burden by paying off royal officials who enjoyed close ties to the local elite. Gálvez was especially alarmed at the situation on the northern frontier, and particularly the Interior Provinces (modern-day Arizona, Sonora, and Sinaloa), where the indigenous Apaches and other tribes eluded colonial rule. In the visitor general's opinion, the sparse Spanish settlement invited foreign colonization at the area, and he noted the advances of Russian settlers in distant Alaska. As Gálvez knew, it would only be a matter of time until either the Russians or the British would lay claim to northwestern New Spain. He also found that the Jesuit order—the wealthiest religious community in the Americas—had taken advantage of this power vacuum to set up autonomous missions on the frontier. On June 24, 1767, just two years after Gálvez arrived in New Spain, Charles III banished the Jesuits from Spain and its colonies.

As Minister of the Indies, Gálvez inaugurated a set of reform measures upon his return to Spain. Collectively known as the Bourbon Reforms, these decrees aimed at maximizing revenue collection and achieving complementary economic development that would guarantee colonial demand for Spanish goods. For instance, the Crown increased the *alcabala*, or sales tax, from 4 to 6 percent. In 1786, Gálvez reorganized colonial administration with a view of achieving more efficient tax collection. Rather than relying on private tax collectors and creole corregidores—the preeminent political and taxing authorities in the countryside—Gálvez established a network of intendants with the nominal charge of assisting the viceroy. Always peninsulares, the intendants replaced creole corregidores with *subdelegados*, many of whom were born in Spain. The king also increased the percentage of peninsular *oidores*, or judges, on the audiencia of Mexico City. In 1750, 51 out of 93 oidores had been creoles; by 1807, however, that number had dropped to 12 out of 99. Finally, Charles III imposed a royal monopoly on tobacco. In total, Crown revenues increased from 3 to 15 million pesos by the end of the eighteenth century.

On balance, the Bourbon Reforms were a mixed bag for the creoles. Many of them benefited from Gálvez's effort to modernize the colonial military. As the Crown launched a concerted attempt to bring the northern frontier under effective control, creoles found well-paid jobs in the expanding army. Nonetheless, creoles resented their higher tax burden as well as the curtailment of their political opportunities in the colonial administration. They believed themselves to be the true Mexicans, descendants of the Spanish conquistadors but linked to the colony's Aztec past by virtue of their birth in Mesoamerica.

The late eighteenth century thus witnessed the emergence of national consciousness: a sense of "Mexico" as a geographical and cultural space distinct from Spain and the other American colonies. In their search for identity and uniqueness, creoles discovered the pre-Columbian civilizations their forebears had conquered and inserted the Aztec "x" into the word "Mexico," which Spaniards had always spelled as "Méjico." The Jesuit friar Francisco Javier Clavijero, a creole from Veracruz, wrote a comprehensive historical study of pre-Columbian Mexico from his exile in Bologna, Italy. Published in 1780, this ten-volume work reconstructed the life of the "Mexicans" on the eve of the conquest, and it particularly emphasized the grandeur of the Aztec and Maya civilizations. Clavijero's interpretation implied that colonialism had violated and diminished Mexico. Several decades later, Fernando de Lizardi wrote his satirical picaresque novel, *El Periquillo Sarniento*, or "the itching parrot," a work that ridiculed colonial corruption and oppression. Creoles also found a unifying figure in the Virgin of Guadalupe. Over time, a cult that had initially served as an instrument of conversion of the indigenous people became a protonational myth that gave creoles, mestizos, and Indians a shared sense of identity.

Events elsewhere in the Atlantic world encouraged the creoles to transform their emerging national consciousness into political action. In 1776, the American Revolution put the Enlightenment ideas of liberty and citizenship into practice, and the newly independent United States provided a model for all Latin Americans tired of Iberian rule. This revolution attacked the ideological foundations of colonial empires, and particularly the divine right of kings. The newly independent United States showed Spanish American creoles that people could take history into their own hands. Next, in 1789, the French Revolution toppled one of Europe's most powerful monarchies to the cry of liberty, equality, and fraternity. Yet these revolutions also provided a warning to Mexican creoles. Both upheavals were destructive and involved international wars and an immense loss of life, but from the creoles' point of view, the American Revolution was greatly preferable to the French one. The American Revolution ended a colonial system but left intact social hierarchies; in contrast, the French Revolution raised the specter of social war, especially during the "great terror" following the executions of Louis XVI and Marie Antoinette in 1792. Even more ominously, the French Revolution encouraged nonwhites in the French colonial empire to seek their freedom. In 1791, Haitian slaves erupted in revolt, expelling the colony's white sugar planter class and creating the Republic of Haiti, only the second independent nation of the Americas and the first to abolish slavery. The Haitian Revolution demonstrated to creoles the social dangers of independence, and it fostered a royalist train of thought that argued for continued colonial rule as the only way to prevent social dissolution.

When the Prussian geologist Alexander von Humboldt arrived in New Spain in 1803 to undertake several months of exploration, the pro- and anti-independence forces among the creoles of New Spain were therefore in a delicate state of balance. Von Humboldt found reasons to be optimistic about the future of the colony. As much as he was astonished by the luxurious world of the silver kings, he believed that Mexico's agricultural potential was even more impressive. But von Humboldt also noted the explosive potential of the social and political differences between the rich and the poor. Influenced by frequent conversations with the creoles of Mexico City, he identified Spanish mismanagement and corruption as the principal obstacles to the colony's reaching its full potential, and he worried that the poor majority might rise up in armed revolt if conditions continued to deteriorate.

Indeed, Spanish rule became more onerous at the turn of the nineteenth century as a consequence of the country's increasing participation in imperial wars. King Charles IV, who ruled from 1788 to 1808, was one of the most incompetent monarchs Spain had ever had. The obtuse Charles was married to his first cousin, the cunning María Luisa of Parma, who ensured that real power in the government lay with the widely despised Prime Minister Manuel de Godoy, who was rumored to be the queen's lover. In addition, Spain faced an increasingly desperate situation in an Atlantic world beset by revolution and warfare. In particular, the French Revolution of 1789 had wide-ranging implications for both Spain and its colonies. When a coalition of monarchs including Charles IV and financed by Great Britain attempted to end the French Revolution by military means, the French raised a massive army by conscripting all men between the ages of 18 and 25. Buoyed by nationalist popular support, this army defeated its enemies and went on the offensive beyond France's borders. After a French army had crossed the Pyrenees, Spain signed a peace treaty with France in 1895, giving up the eastern part of the island of Hispaniola (the present-day Dominican Republic). Fearful of further setbacks, Charles agreed to join France in an alliance against Great Britain in 1796. At first glance, this alliance appeared well chosen: under Napoleon Bonaparte, the most capable military officer in the revolutionary army, the French scored impressive victories. In 1802, Napoleon was crowned emperor. Five years later, the Low Countries, Switzerland, Italy, and much of Germany were under his control. But the war with England had repercussions for Spain's colonial empire. At war with the world's preeminent naval power, Spain found its main port of Cádiz blockaded by the British until 1800, and in 1805, the British navy defeated the combined French and Spanish forces at Trafalgar.

To face these crises, the Spanish prime minister Godoy attempted to increase revenue collection from the colonies. He drastically raised the price of *mayorazgo*, or entail, a concession necessary to obtain noble status or pass wealth from one generation on to the next. Godoy also demanded forced loans from merchant and artisan guilds in the colonies. In December 1804, the Law of Consolidation expropriated funds held by the religious confraternities, the *cofradías*, a move that took away the small savings that indigenous communities had accumulated in the name of the Church. The decree also seized the mortgages and loans of the Church, the principal moneylender in New Spain, as well as the land and real estate purchased with those funds. The Law of Consolidation threatened both creoles and indigenous communities with financial ruin, and it even angered peninsulares, many of whom were in debt to the Church as well. Thus, Godoy's efforts to extract maximum revenue from the Spanish colonies galvanized opposition to colonial rule among both the elites and the lower classes. By 1807—the year Napoleon readied an invasion force for the Iberian peninsula—the seeds of the Wars of Independence had been sown.

Yet independence had to be carefully considered in an age in which the newly sovereign United States sought to expand its borders westward toward New Spain. In 1803, Napoleon sold the vast territory of Louisiana to the United States, creating a land border between that country and New Spain. For Mexicans, this was a bad omen that presaged conflicts with the United States in the decade ahead.

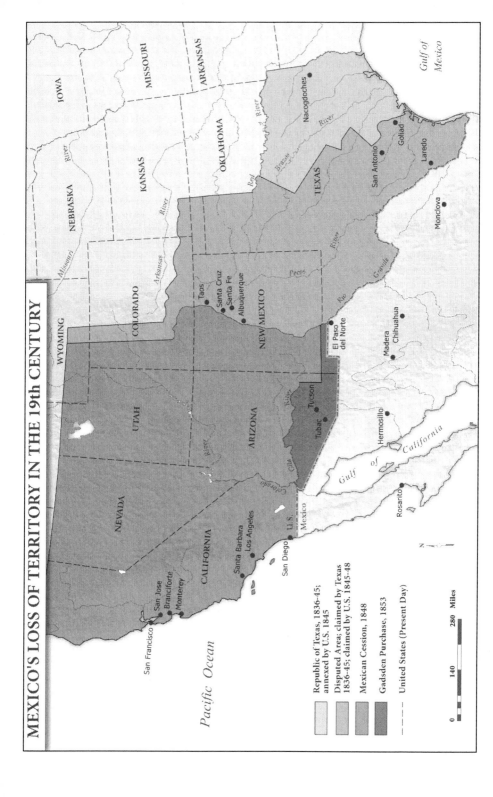

MEXICO'S LOSS OF TERRITORY IN THE 19th CENTURY

Legend:
- Republic of Texas, 1836–45; annexed by U.S. 1845
- Disputed Area; claimed by Texas 1836–45; claimed by U.S. 1845–48
- Mexican Cession, 1848
- Gadsden Purchase, 1853
- – – – United States (Present Day)

0   140   280 Miles

IOWA
MISSOURI
ARKANSAS
NEBRASKA
KANSAS
OKLAHOMA
WYOMING
COLORADO
NEW MEXICO
UTAH
ARIZONA
NEVADA
CALIFORNIA
TEXAS

Missouri River
Arkansas River
Red River
Brazos River
Pecos River
Rio Grande
Gila River
Colorado River

Nacogdoches
San Antonio
Goliad
Laredo
Monclova
Taos
Santa Cruz
Santa Fe
Albuquerque
El Paso del Norte
Madera
Chihuahua
Tucson
Tubac
Hermosillo
Rosarito
San Diego
Los Angeles
Santa Barbara
Monterey
Branciforte
San Jose
San Francisco

U.S.
Mexico

Pacific Ocean
Gulf of Mexico
Gulf of California

CHAPTER TWO

❧ Independence ❧
and Upheaval

On the early morning of September 16, 1810, Father Miguel Hidalgo y Costilla rang the bells of the parish church of the town of Dolores, Guanajuato,
to summon his flock to mass. It was a most unusual hour: dawn had not yet
broken, and most of his parishioners looked at him tired and bleary-eyed. His
audience included mestizos as well as indigenous campesinos from Dolores and
neighboring villages. But Hidalgo did not have an ordinary sermon in mind.
He formed part of a group of conspirators against the Spanish Crown, and
just a few hours before, fellow rebel Juan de Aldama had warned Hidalgo of
his impending arrest. Although the text of his speech has not survived, among
the lines attributed to Hidalgo were: "Long live our Virgin of Guadalupe!
Death to bad government! Death to the *gachupines*!" All Mexican schoolchildren still learn Hidalgo's fervent invocation to his followers, albeit without
the above-mentioned death threats, deleted for the sake of good taste and
citizenship. This oration—a speech known today as the *grito de Dolores*, or Cry
of Dolores—inaugurated a long series of wars that ultimately freed Mexico
from its colonial masters.

The road to nationhood, however, was a difficult one. Hidalgo could
not have imagined the chaos his movement would help unleash. The Wars
of Independence ushered in a degree of death and destruction not seen
since the Spanish conquest and its aftermath. Even after the achievement of
independence, political stability remained elusive, and war—both civil and
foreign—was the hallmark of the early national period. Political allegiances
remained local and regional rather than national, and the caudillos, powerful
regional warlords, contested for power. Between 1821 and 1867, rival factions
fought for supremacy, without clearly defined political goals. At first, these

factions called themselves "Centralist" and "Federalist," before coalescing into the "Conservative" and "Liberal" parties. Almost fifty governments ruled Mexico between 1821 and 1867, and coups d'état rather than elections defined most presidential terms. At several junctures, it appeared as if Mexico would break apart into several smaller units, just as Gran Colombia had given way to the independent republics of Colombia, Ecuador, and Venezuela. Such a breakup would not have surprised anyone, as the new nation united several separate kingdoms and colonial administrations. As a result, Central America seceded from Mexico in 1823 after a brief union; Texas, in 1836; and in the 1840s, Yucatán threatened to do the same. On four different occasions, foreign armies invaded Mexican soil. The most serious of these invasions, the war with the United States (1846–48), resulted in the U.S. annexation of half of Mexico's territory. The unrest also produced a long economic crisis. Central Mexico's prolonged warfare led to a shutdown of many of the silver mines, the mainstay of the colonial economy. In the absence of workers, the mines flooded, which rendered them useless for production until late in the century when electric pumps allowed the removal of water on a large scale. In addition, the political unrest impeded overland trade, as caudillos and bandits often intercepted long-distance shipments. In light of this prolonged time of troubles, it is surprising that nineteenth-century Mexico remained one nation.

THE WARS OF INDEPENDENCE, 1810-1821

Considered the father of the independence movement, Hidalgo was born in 1753, the son of an hacienda administrator. He studied Latin grammar and rhetoric in a Jesuit school until the expulsion of that order when he was fourteen years old; then he went to study arts and theology at the Real y Pontífica Universidad de México, the preeminent university of the colony. Ordained as a priest in 1778, he began a career in higher education at the College of San Nicolás in Valladolid, Michoacán, the present-day city of Morelia. At the same time his family came into money and landownership, however, Hidalgo dove headlong into trouble. As rector of San Nicolás, he drew the ire of ecclesiastical authorities due to his unorthodox and innovative teaching methods, his penchant for gambling, and the fact that he had three children with two different women. Dismissed from his post in 1792, Hidalgo became an interim curate, spending his free time reading the works of French Enlightenment authors. This was not a lucrative profession, as Hidalgo was merely filling in for a parish priest, who continued to enjoy most of the financial benefits of that office. In 1803, Hidalgo obtained the curacy of Dolores upon the death of his elder brother. He viewed this as an opportunity to become a local entrepreneur, introducing to the area new industries such as tanning, tile making, and wine producing. Just when he believed he had turned the corner financially, however, the Law of Consolidation forced immediate repayment on the mortgages he had secured to invest in these ventures. Even worse, in 1807 the Inquisition, which already kept a thick file on Hidalgo that documented his earlier transgressions, investigated him for criticizing Catholic orthodoxy and the Spanish Crown.

By then, chaos had broken out in the Spanish Empire. In 1807, Napoleon's troops had invaded Spain on their way to occupying Portugal, then an ally of Great Britain. En route, French forces seized several Spanish cities, adding to the political turmoil within the monarchy that had persisted since Charles IV's accession to the throne. In March 1808, Charles abdicated in favor of his oldest son and heir, Ferdinand VII. In hopes of consolidating his position, Ferdinand turned to Napoleon, who promptly imprisoned Ferdinand and forced his abdication. In place of Ferdinand, Napoleon named his own brother, Joseph Bonaparte, the king of Spain and its colonies. Many Spanish subjects did not accept the imposition of Joseph, and creoles throughout Spanish America pledged their loyalty to Ferdinand. In this fashion, the creoles subverted colonialism by arguing that they were subjects of the king, just like the peninsulares, and as such equal in all respects to the Spaniards. The creoles of Mexico City thus used their support of the institution of monarchy to defend the principle of popular sovereignty during meetings of a *cabildo abierto*, or open city council. In July 1808, such a cabildo abierto attended by many of the city's wealthy creole males petitioned Viceroy José de Iturrigaray—a leader hated for his ruthlessness in enforcing the Crown's attempts at revenue collection. The cabildo asked the viceroy to form a council composed of representatives of the largest cities in New Spain in order to address the void in colonial leadership. Iturrigaray hesitated but agreed to convene a meeting of notable leaders from Mexico City only. Incensed over the viceroy's concession to the creoles, the peninsulares staged a coup d'état and overthrew Iturrigaray. This coup challenged the legality of colonial administration and set a longstanding precedent by which political power derived from the force of arms rather than the law. It also brought chaos to the viceregal palace, as Iturrigaray's two successors were exceptionally weak leaders who never enjoyed any real authority. By 1810, the quarrelsome audiencia of Mexico City had assumed the functions of the viceroy.

This dual power vacuum in Madrid and in Mexico City created an opening for lesser creoles such as Hidalgo, who embraced Ferdinand as a convenient figurehead for his own movement for greater autonomy. In 1810, Hidalgo joined a circle that included other free-thinking creoles such as Juan de Aldama, Ignacio Allende, Epigmenio González, and Josefa Ortiz de Domínguez, the wife of the local corregidor who would come to be known in history as *la corregidora*. The group planned a coup d'état in the name of Ferdinand—a coup that would have broken out on December 8, 1810, if one of the conspirators had not informed the colonial authorities. On September 13, the Crown's men barged into Domínguez's house and found a large supply of weapons and ammunition. Informed by her husband, Ortiz relayed the news to Hidalgo, who—together with Aldama and Allende—decided to begin the rebellion at once.

The rebellion united Hidalgo and his creole co-conspirators, who were steeped in Enlightenment thought, with a constituency very different from them: the local campesinos and workers, who were looking to fight their way out of poverty. As a steady companion for most Mexican campesinos throughout the colonial period, poverty had greatly increased in Guanajuato and many other regions, the result of the rapid population growth in the eighteenth century. This population growth contributed to an associated rise in food prices. From the outset, the larger, uneducated, and impoverished constituency gained the upper hand, and Hidalgo's revolt found an enthusiastic reception in rural Guanajuato. Thousands of campesinos, many of them indigenous, flocked to Hidalgo's cause, and the priest suddenly and unexpectedly found himself at the head of a popular army.

To unite his disparate movement, Hidalgo embraced an important unifying symbol already alluded to in his grito. On his march toward the city of San Miguel, he picked up a banner of the Virgin of Guadalupe in a church and proclaimed her the symbol of his rebellion. By the end of that day, Hidalgo's forces had seized San Miguel, the first major town captured by the rebels. The banner of Guadalupe brought even greater popular support to the movement.

With this first victory, the priest who, unfortunately, had never received military training, began to lose his leadership over the movement. Eager to exact revenge for centuries of abuse upon the city's creole inhabitants, the motley army began to pillage San Miguel before Hidalgo's ally Allende was able to restore a semblance of order. The following day, the mob got out of control, now subjecting the city of Celaya to the type of destruction that Allende had just stopped in San Miguel. On September 28, Hidalgo's popular army approached the famous silver city of Guanajuato, one of the wealthiest cities in the Spanish Empire. The military commander of Guanajuato had heard of the destruction in Celaya and refused to surrender the city, instead concentrating the population in his city's granary, the Alhóndiga de Granaditas. The rebels, however, would not be denied. They set the wooden door of the granary on fire, stormed the building, and killed most of the people inside. Much of the ruling class of the silver city died a cruel death that day. (One of the young boys witnessing his father's death was Lucas Alamán, who would gain fame as the preeminent conservative statesman and historian of the early independence years.) A month later, Hidalgo's forces won another decisive and bloody victory at Monte de las Cruces near Mexico City.

That victory, however, proved to be Hidalgo's last. Within striking distance of the ultimate prize—the seizure of Mexico City—the priest had second thoughts about pressing onward. He feared a repetition of the awful events in Guanajuato, which had upset him deeply. He remembered that he, too, was a creole and could not countenance the idea of a mob destroying Mexico City. Moreover, his forces had sustained heavy losses during the previous battles. Therefore, Hidalgo decided to retreat rather than press on toward the capital. As a result, the royalist forces won enough time to obtain reinforcements, and thousands of Hidalgo's troops deserted his army, disappointed at the waffling of their leader. In January 1811, the Spanish forces of General Félix Calleja devastated the rebel army. Two months later, Hidalgo was arrested and handed over to the Inquisition, which sentenced him to death by firing squad. The sentence was carried out on July 30, 1811, but only after Hidalgo had handed out candies to his executioners. Whether Hidalgo intended to show forgiveness or cement his future as a martyr is unclear. Soon thereafter, the Spaniards displayed his severed head—along with those of Aldama, Allende, and other rebel leaders—on pikes on the wall of the Alhóndiga in Guanajuato as a warning to any other would-be independence fighters.

After Hidalgo's death, the leadership of the rebels fell to another priest, José María Morelos y Pavón. Unlike Hidalgo, Morelos was a mestizo and a brilliant military strategist. Aware that the Hidalgo revolt had scared the creoles into submission to colonial rule, Morelos pursued a different strategy of insurrection. He knew that the poor majority constituted the backbone of his rebellion, and he relied on the use of guerrilla attacks, shying away from any direct engagement with Calleja's army. He was also aware of the continuing tensions between Spain and its colonists. In 1812, the Cortes de Cádiz, a government set up in Spain to oppose Joseph (the king of Spain) at a time when Napoleon's energies were concentrated on the vain enterprise of conquering Russia, promulgated a liberal constitution guaranteeing basic civil rights and equality before the law. The chaos in Spain weakened the resolve of the royalists to defeat the insurrection, and that same year, Morelos's guerrillas in the New World managed to encircle Mexico City. At the same time, however, the constitution also gave creoles the idea that reform was possible in cooperation with Spain. In response to this challenge, Morelos demonstrated that he—unlike Hidalgo—pursued clear political goals. In September 1813, he convened the Congress of Chilpancingo, which announced the formal independence of Mexico. The Congress also adopted Mexico's first national constitution, a document that promised to redress some of the worst abuses committed against the poor majority. At a time when slavery remained legal in the United States, the Mexican delegates decreed the abolition of slavery and debt servitude. They also called for an end to the fueros, the extralegal privileges enjoyed by the Church and the army.

Yet despite his popular appeal, Morelos ultimately suffered the same fate as Hidalgo. The peninsulares and creoles, afraid of mob violence, closed ranks, preferring continued colonial rule over Morelos' rebellion, which they viewed as chaos. In 1814, Spain once again fell under Bourbon rule following the defeat of Napoleon. The newly installed King Ferdinand VII sent reinforcements to New Spain. Thus assured of royal support, General Calleja went on the offensive and broke the guerrilla's encirclement of the capital. Although Morelos managed to reconvene his supporters in Apatzingán, Michoacán, to enshrine the principles of his movement in the first national constitution of Mexico, he now witnessed the flip side of his guerrilla strategy. Without a home base controlled by his forces, he was on the run from the Crown, and in late 1815, the royalists captured him. Like Hidalgo, Morelos was tried by the Inquisition, condemned to death, and handed over to secular authorities. After his execution on December 22, 1815, his severed head joined Hidalgo's on a pike on the wall of the Alhóndiga. Among those who hunted down Morelos was a creole royalist of aristocratic provenance named Agustín de Iturbide.

For the next five years there was a prolonged stalemate between the remnants of Morelos's guerrilla and the royalist forces. The Crown could not defeat the rebels, and two new leaders—Guadalupe Victoria in Puebla and Veracruz, and Vicente Guerrero in Oaxaca—commanded formidable rebel forces. Over time, Mexicans from all walks of life grew weary of the warfare, noticing the economic effects of war. As is often the case in history, the army of occupation became increasingly unpopular, while nativist and xenophobic sentiment increased. However, neither Victoria nor Guerrero could expand their pockets of resistance, and it is likely that the stalemate would have continued if not for events in Spain. The Bourbon Ferdinand, desiring to rule in absolutist fashion as had his ancestors, disavowed his earlier pledge to accept the liberal Constitution of 1812. In 1820, just as the king prepared to send a massive force to the Americas to suppress the revolts for independence raging not only in New Spain but also in Venezuela and Argentina, liberal army leaders in Spain staged a coup d'état that demanded Ferdinand's compliance with the constitution promulgated by the Cortes de Cádiz eight years before.

This coup changed the complexion of the war in New Spain. Creole royalists like Iturbide feared the consequences of lower-class revolts such as those witnessed under Hidalgo's and Morelos's leadership. He desired nothing more than to preserve the elitist social order in the colony. But from firsthand experience, Iturbide knew that he could not defeat Guerrero and Victoria, and he was aware that many royalist creoles had become weary of the war. Also, Iturbide had spent much of the period from 1816 to 1820 unemployed, as his reputation as an excessively cruel commander during the campaigns against the Morelos insurgency had resulted in the termination of his command over the royalist forces in Guanajuato and Valladolid. Hence, the outcry over the liberal coup in Spain gave Iturbide the perfect pretext to pay back his former employers by making common cause with the enemy.

On February 24, 1821, Iturbide and Guerrero announced the Plan of Iguala, which proclaimed Mexico's independence and postulated the new nation as a constitutional monarchy. This plan, like the many subsequent ones in the course of Mexican history, was an announcement by military leaders containing a political progam for the nation. The throne of the new nation would be offered to Ferdinand VII, one of his three sons, or any other person designated by the Mexican Cortes, or parliament. Subsequently, most attempted coups d'état would feature such a plan, usually with lofty language and promises for sweeping social and political change. Compared with later such plans, or even the proclamations of Morelos, the Plan of Iguala was modest. Designed to avoid upsetting the social structure, it contained three simple provisions: a) equal treatment under law for peninsulares and creoles; b) Catholicism as the official religion; and c) the independence of Mexico under a moderate monarchy. These provisions—*unión, religión,* and *independencia*—became known as the Three Guarantees, and the combined forces of Iturbide, Guerrero, and Victoria called themselves the *ejército trigarante,* or the Army of the Three Guarantees. These three guarantees are represented by the three colors on the Mexican flag. Red stands for the union of America and Europe, that is, the blood of creoles and peninsulares; white, for the purity of the Catholic faith; and green, for the hope of independence. The Trigarante army overwhelmed the colonial authorities. On September 27, 1821, the rebels occupied Mexico City, and the viceroy and his court fled to Spain. Mexico was an independent country.

This triumph, however, bore a problematic legacy. The new rulers did not embody many of the ideals for which the rebels had shed their blood during ten years of warfare. Independence had arrived through the caprice and deception of Iturbide, a creole military leader who had made his career fighting the popular armies of Morelos and Guerrero. Iturbide's about-face and subsequent pact with the very men he had been paid to defeat set an unfortunate precedent for Mexican history. He demonstrated the primacy of opportunism and self-interest and the expediency of political principles. Against the backdrop of a devastated economy in a country that had produced less than 25 percent of the silver mined the year before the Hidalgo revolt, the political strife was ominous.

The victors of the newly independent Mexico did not share a common vision for the nation. After the American Revolution resulted in the formation of the United States, the basic form of government of the new nation—a republic with a division of power among a president, Congress, and independent judiciary—was never in doubt. The politicians of the early republic squabbled over the extent of federal versus state power as well as the terms of incorporation of any future territorial annexations. Postindependence Mexico, on the other hand, featured both monarchists and republicans. Allies of Iturbide, the former group desired to elevate a European prince to a Mexican throne. Even though they had signed on to the Plan of Iguala that declared Mexico to be a monarchy, however, Guerrero, Victoria, and others advocated a parliamentary democracy molded in accordance with the U.S. model.

THE SEARCH FOR STABILITY, 1821–1854

Independence, of course, did not guarantee lasting peace. Iturbide himself provided perhaps the greatest indicator of future trouble when he confused the new nation's interests with his own. As presiding officer of a provisional junta that governed Mexico, Iturbide instituted for himself a new military title, *Generalísimo de Tierra y Mar* (highest general of the earth and sea), as well as an annual salary in the exorbitant amount of 180,000 pesos. But even that designation and remuneration did not sufficiently flatter the general's vanity. On May 18, 1822, Iturbide's troops marched through the streets demanding his coronation as Agustín I of Mexico. After a brief moment of feigning reluctance to accept this high honor—a ritual befitting a monarch—Iturbide agreed to be

Mexico's first emperor since the Aztec ruler Cuauhtémoc. On July 21, 1822, he was coronated amidst great fanfare. His ascension to the throne signified that political rule in Mexico remained personal in nature, and that loyalty to the new emperor had substituted for the old allegiance to the Spanish Crown. It appeared that very little had changed with independence.

Iturbide's coronation flattered his ego but pleased no one else. Monarchists had desired to elevate a European prince to the Mexican throne, while republicans had remained determined to establish a parliamentary system. During his eighteen short months in power, the flamboyant and arrogant emperor alienated his supporters in Mexico City. Those farther away simply ignored or openly disavowed him: for example, in early 1823 the Central American states, which had joined Iturbide in the Plan of Iguala, broke free from Mexico. So weak was Iturbide's hold on power that the first U.S. diplomatic envoy in Mexico City, Joel R. Poinsett, openly lobbied for the U.S. annexation of vast stretches of the Mexican north without losing his accreditation. In the end, however, Poinsett was unsuccessful and returned to his native South Carolina, his only souvenir the flowery plant that still bears his name. Alarmed about the prospect of U.S. annexations, Iturbide invited English-speaking farmers to settle in Texas as long as they promised to respect Mexican law and practice Catholicism. This attempt to forge an Anglo-Catholic buffer between the United States and Mexico finalized plans that dated from the late colonial period. In fact, however, many Anglo settlers who had converted to Catholicism continued the Protestant traditions in which they had been raised.

An even greater problem for Iturbide was the deepening economic crisis following independence. The destruction of silver mining left the national currency without support. Those who could take money out of Mexico and invest it elsewhere readily did so. In addition, agricultural production had declined dramatically during the years of guerrilla warfare, and as a result, food prices rose steadily. Finally, Iturbide's army of 80,000 comprised almost 40,000 officers, whose salaries drained whatever was left in the treasury. As if these problems were not bad enough, Iturbide soured his supporters by his use of nepotism and penchant for ridiculous pomp. He not only awarded noble titles to his family, but he also decreed that the birthdays of his immediate family members be celebrated as national holidays. Like an Old World monarch, he ordered subjects who wished to see him to kneel and kiss his hand.

In the end, however, it was not pomp but repression that spelled the end of Iturbide's empire. His rule was authoritarian, and dissent was not tolerated. For example, in August 1822, the emperor discovered a conspiracy involving several distinguished creoles in Congress. In response, he arrested its ringleaders, Fray Servando Teresa de Mier and Carlos María de Bustamante. After Congress protested against this act, Iturbide dissolved the legislature on October 31, 1822—the first of many Mexican heads of state to abolish a legislative branch that had opposed them. In refusing to respect the autonomy of Congress, Iturbide thus set a precedent that would plague Mexico for the rest of the nineteenth century. He also served as a role model for his authoritarian successors both at the national and the regional levels.

Iturbide's action elicited widespread outcry among influential creoles such as the military commander of Veracruz, a man by the name of Antonio de Padua María Severino López de Santa Anna y Pérez de Lebrón. The name was a mouthful, and most Mexicans knew him simply as "Santa Anna," their most influential leader during the three decades following independence. Born in Jalapa, Veracruz, in 1794 to Spanish parents, Santa Anna had begun his career in the army in 1810 and served with the royalist forces until 1821, when he proclaimed his adherence to the Plan of Iguala. By that time, he had become a successful land- and businessowner in the Jalapa region of Veracruz, and he commanded a private army that controlled that strategically important region located along the route from the port of Veracruz to Mexico City. An opportunist par excellence, Santa Anna always anticipated the shifting political winds. Thus he decided that Iturbide's days in power were numbered, and on December 1, 1822, Santa Anna proclaimed Mexico a republic in his Plan de Veracruz. Soon thereafter, Guerrero and Victoria joined this plan, and the spreading revolt forced Iturbide to step down from his throne. In March 1823, the rebels took Mexico City to the jubilant acclaim of the city's inhabitants, and Mexico became a republic. Guadalupe Victoria and two of his closest associates formed a three-man junta until a president could be elected.

Nonetheless, this victory did not end the strife. As their first significant act in office, Victoria and his allies charged a constituent assembly with the task of drafting a federal constitution. The convention met for the first time on November 27, and within a few days, delegates had divided into two hostile camps. A Centralist faction coalesced around Mier and Bustamante, the leaders of the congressional opposition to Iturbide. Seeing themselves as the heirs of Hispanic political traditions, the Centralists advocated a strong central government and a significant political role of the Catholic Church. Their rivals were the Federalists around Victoria who drew their political lessons from the example of the United States. Desiring to emulate Anglo American political traditions, the Federalists wanted a weak central government, strong, autonomous states, and an end to the privileges of the Church. Ultimately, the Federalists prevailed on issues of political organization, and the Constitution of 1824 largely resembled its U.S. counterpart with a system of shared government and a bicameral Congress. Nonetheless, the Centralists emerged victorious on three significant issues: Catholicism remained the state religion; the president could invoke special executive powers in case of an emergency; and the colonial fueros remained (special privileges that allowed members of the clergy and army to stand trial in separate courts). It was an explosive compromise that satisfied no one, and the convention had exposed the principal political fault lines of the early republic.

An Anglo American political system such as the one reflected in the Constitution of 1824 faced daunting obstacles in a socially, regionally, and ethnically divided Mexico. The decade of fighting had destroyed an incipient large-scale distribution network of goods, people, and ideas, and Mexicans were more isolated from each other than they had been in the late colonial period. Outside the capital, most Mexicans expressed allegiance to their region rather than their nation, especially since the social and political order of that nation safeguarded the interests of the privileged classes in the capital. Mexico remained a rural country, and over a third of the population was indigenous. Most of the indigenous people lived in small villages, or *pueblos*, having limited contact with surrounding areas. Rural towns featured a mix of indigenous people and mestizos. The inhabitants of these towns felt the authority of the central government only in negative ways, such as by taxation and the much-feared *leva*, or military draft. Only in Mexico City and other large cities did observers find any sense of national identity, and even within those cities, sharp social distinctions divided the rich from the poor. Urban Mexicans thought in terms of three different social classes. The *gente alta*, the "high people," or elite, consisted of the property owners. The *gente decente*, the "decent people," or middle class, included both professionals and artisans. Finally, the *gente humilde*, the "humble people," or poor, included the urban workers and beggars. A derogatory term widely used to describe the beggars was *léperos*, or lepers. Class identity had strong cultural elements: while the gente alta pursued a formal education and aspired to mimic European ways, the gente humilde engaged in an everyday struggle for survival. Like the vast majority of rural inhabitants (and almost all women), the urban poor remained illiterate. Thus, when Mexican politicians wrote lofty programs and political plans, they addressed a tiny, wealthy, urban, and almost exclusively male audience.

To make matters worse, foreigners continued to play important roles in nineteenth-century Mexico. To be sure, Spanish colonial rule had ended with the triumph of Iturbide. But at least initially, the peninsulares continued to control petty commerce, and Spanish priests occupied important positions in the Church hierarchy. British banks held much of the nation's foreign debt, and European merchants—especially Spanish, British, and French traders—dominated wholesale commerce, particularly in the imported clothes and luxury items craved by the gente alta and the gente decente.

In light of these divisions, it is not surprising that clientelist relationships trumped political ideas and partisanship. Clientelism denotes the practice of using ties of family, marriage, and friendship to forge important economic and political networks. In Mexico, as in the rest of Latin America, caudillos (regional military leaders), had emerged during the Wars of Independence. With the help of military forces at their personal command, these caudillos vied for power after the disintegration of Spanish colonial rule. Their power rested on charisma and personal alliances in which the caudillos promised a material benefit to their followers (clients), who reciprocated by pledging loyalty to their leader. In turn, the allies of the caudillo passed on some of this material benefit to their own clients, again in exchange for their loyalty and support. Many of these followers were called caciques, or local bosses, a term used in adaptation of the Náhuatl word for a village chief. The caciques often, but not always, held formal political offices such as that of mayor or *jefe político*. On the national scene, the caudillos viewed the Centralist and Federalist factions as mere vehicles for their ambitions, and many of them easily changed political affiliation.

Among the first generation of political leaders of the new republic, some of the foremost caudillos were Santa Anna and Vicente Guerrero, relatively uneducated military leaders who enjoyed large personal followings. Another important caudillo, Juan Alvarez, ruled virtually unchallenged over southern Mexico for more than five decades. All three of these caudillos had large followings in their regions—followings that accepted the mandates of their caudillos over those of the federal government. The trouble for the first president of republican Mexico, Guadalupe Victoria, was that the caudillos did not respect the newly created political institutions. In their minds, it was they who had won independence on the battlefield, and they were not about to be subordinated by city slickers under the guise of parliamentary procedures. As Victoria found out, Santa Anna was a particularly significant adversary. His appeal stemmed from his military stature, but also from his success as a business- and landowner. In addition, the caudillo of Veracruz also found adherents as the embodiment of antipolitics—someone who wanted nothing to do with Centralists, Federalists, and well-dressed, bureaucratic politicians from the city in general. In that fashion, Santa Anna resembled South American caudillos such as José Antonio Páez of Venezuela and Juan Manuel de Rosas of Argentina. Thus Victoria confronted the same political and economic problems that had proven Iturbide's undoing, and the president never exerted effective control over most of the national territory. In 1827, his vice president, Nicolás Bravo, staged an unsuccessful coup against him, and the following year his own party demonstrated its lack of respect for democracy when it refused to recognize the triumph of the opposition in the presidential elections. Aided by Santa Anna, they imposed Guerrero as the second president of Mexico. With Guerrero, the caudillos had reached the presidency.

Guerrero had hardly uttered the oath of office when he learned that Spain had launched an attempt to repossess its former colony. In July 1829—one year after the remainder of Spanish South America had attained independence—General Isidro Barradas launched an invasion from Cuba, one of the three last Spanish colonies in the Americas along with the Dominican Republic and Puerto Rico. Barradas' forces seized the northeastern port town of Tampico but got no further. In August, Santa Anna's forces laid siege to Tampico and took the city two months later. Afraid of reprisals, most of the remaining Spaniards fled Mexico after the failed invasion. With this exodus, the majority of all retail merchants had left the country. British, French, and German traders filled the gap in wholesale commerce, accentuating Mexico's dependence on what would be the rising European industrial powers of the nineteenth century. The Spanish exodus also capped a decade of capital flight that left the government starved of significant sources of revenue until the rebuilding of the mining economy in the 1880s.

The Spanish invasion inaugurated the heyday of Santa Anna. In the words of Lucas Alamán, one of the survivors of Hidalgo's assault on the Alhóndiga and a foremost politician of this era, postindependence Mexican political history was the history of Santa Anna's revolutions. As the linchpin of both the anti-Iturbide alliance and the coup that elevated Guerrero to the presidency, Santa Anna emerged as the most important leader of the new republic, and he soon demonstrated his ability to transcend the Centralist/Federalist conflict by his own, extensive clientelist network. He had an uncanny ability to portray himself as the defender of his fatherland. His role in repelling the Spanish attempt at reconquest earned him the reputation of a defender of national sovereignty. In 1832, he allied with the Federalists in a successful coup against President Anastasio Bustamante and became president (for the first time) on May 16, 1833, serving just eighteen days until June 3, 1833, when he stepped aside in favor of Vice President Valentín Gómez Farías, a radical Liberal who desired to end all privileges of the Church and army in Mexico. Just a few months later, Gómez Farías's anticlerical reforms led Santa Anna to reverse his stance and return to the presidency in alliance with the Centralists. Thus began a pattern in which Santa Anna occupied and relinquished the presidency eleven times; his longest term was his last, which lasted almost twenty-eight months (April 1853–August 1855). Most of the time, he enjoyed his role as a power behind the scenes who came to the fore whenever he believed the nation needed him. For example, in 1836; he gained fame in leading Mexican troops at the battle of the Alamo during the war that led to the independence of Texas. Two years later, in 1838, he coordinated the defense of Mexico against a French invasion force sent to collect debts owed to French residents, including a baker in Mexico City who had once lost his pastries to a marauding mob. During what French journalists later dubbed the Pastry War, Santa Anna lost his left leg to a cannon shot, and in 1842, astonishingly, he gave his leg a state burial with a twelve-gun salute. Even more bizarre, two years later, one of Santa Anna's many presidencies ended in a coup that resulted in the victors digging out his leg from its mausoleum and waving it through the streets.

Although many historians have attributed Santa Anna's success to the chaos of the postindependence decades, his ability to dominate Mexican politics over a period of twenty-five years requires a different explanation. In fact, opportunism alone could not have guided a leader through a political universe ordered by chaos; hence, historian Frank Tannenbaum's assessment of Santa Anna as "the evil genius of Mexico's destiny" misses its mark. Instead, Mexicans repeatedly called upon Santa Anna's leadership because there was no one else, and because the caudillo vowed to defend the interests of the propertied classes even as he opposed and ridiculed their intellectual representatives. Santa Anna was steadfast in both his support of the social order and in his folksy defense of antipolitics. He also personified Mexican nationalism: as evidenced by his role in defeating the Spanish attempt at re-conquest as well as numerous acts of bravery and military successes against enemies both domestic and foreign.

Despite Santa Anna's efforts to unify the nation, he and other Mexican leaders could not prevent U.S. land grabbing. In 1835, Santa Anna abrogated the Constitution of 1824 and imposed Centralist rule upon Mexico, the "Seven Laws" that antagonized many inhabitants of the distant frontier. The abrogation of the constitution gave the Anglo American settlers in Texas an opportunity they had long been looking for, and under the leadership of Stephen F. Austin and Sam Houston, they took up arms under the banner of independence following the devastating defeat of Santa Anna's army at San

Jacinto, the Texans easily triumphed over the Mexican forces. In 1836, the "Lone Star Republic" was born, and eight years later Texas was admitted to the Union. The U.S. annexation of Texas in 1845 sparked one of the many instances in which Santa Anna left the presidency, overthrown by a coup d'état that ended with him in exile.

Disputes over the Texas-Mexico border, in particular the question of whether the Rio Grande or the Nueces River formed the proper boundary, resulted in further complications with the United States. The issue was not a small one, as the U.S. claim doubled the size of Texas to include not only San Antonio but also Albuquerque, the present state capital of New Mexico. To enforce this claim, U.S. President James K. Polk sent envoy John Slidell to negotiate with the Mexican government. Slidell carried instructions to secure the border claimed by the Texans, as well as to make an offer to buy California and the rest of New Mexico for a grand total of $30 million. Confident that its army, which matched the U.S. military forces in size, would repel an invasion, the Mexican government sent Slidell packing. Polk's response was to send a U.S. contingent under General Zachary Taylor across the Nueces River at Corpus Christi. After Mexican troops killed several of Taylor's troops, the U.S. Congress declared war. Thereafter, Taylor's army slowly wound its way south, occupying the strategically significant city of Monterrey and taking control over the northeast. Farther west, U.S. forces scored easy victories and reached the city of Chihuahua and the Pacific coast at San Diego. The shocking course of the war revealed the ineptitude of the Mexican army, as its commanders were far more interested in battling for the presidency than in repelling the invaders. It was time, once again, for Santa Anna to save the nation. In 1846, he reassumed the presidency.

The worst, however, was yet to come. Near Saltillo, Coahuila, Santa Anna failed to dislodge the U.S. forces in February 1847, and three weeks later General Winfield Scott's Army of Occupation landed near Veracruz and invaded the heartland from the same direction that had brought Cortés success more than three hundred years earlier. On September 13, Scott's troops occupied the capital. The last stand came on Chapultepec Hill, where six Mexican cadets, still remembered as the *niños héroes*, or boy heroes, fell to their deaths rather than surrender to the North Americans, also known to Mexicans as *gringos*. Except for some guerrilla warfare in Veracruz, the war had ended. On February 2, 1848, the Mexican government signed the Treaty of Guadalupe Hidalgo, in which the nation ceded half of its territory to the United States, including the present-day states of California, Nevada, Arizona, and New Mexico as well as parts of Colorado, Texas, and Utah. The war with the United States marked an important turning point in ways other than these tremendous territorial losses, which involved vast, if sparsely populated, areas. The invasion also brought many Mexicans living in the ceded lands into first-time contact with the people and culture of the United States, and particularly the Protestant religions, Anglo American food, and industrially manufactured products. Finally, U.S. land grabbing in the north served as a clarion call to all Mexican leaders to set aside their differences. The defeat left a deep wound in the hearts of nationalists, and many political leaders vowed never again to let foreigners exploit internal dissensions for their own benefit.

Events in the southeast—and particularly the Yucatán peninsula—sounded an equally dire warning. In 1847, even as Mexico waged war with the United States, Yucatán's Maya campesinos revolted against the white elite in the largest and most serious regional uprising in modern Mexican history. As had happened before, squabbles among the elite created an opening for an oppressed group to express its grievances. Dubbed the Caste War, the revolt brought the Maya troops to the cusp of conquering the Yucatán state capital of Mérida. The state government regrouped and defeated the rebels, who finally sought refuge in the peninsula's abundant woods and shrublands, where they continued to organize under the banner of Chan Santa Cruz, or the Cult of the Speaking Cross. It was not until the Mexican Revolution that government forces finally crushed the rebellion, although isolated fighting continued into the 1930s. Along with the Yaquis in Sonora, who fought a virtually endless series of wars to keep their land and autonomy until their defeat in the late phases of the Mexican Revolution, Maya resistance proved one of the most successful and persistent indigenous challenges to central authority.

This example not only showed the strength of indigenous resistance, but it also demonstrated the regional character of Mexican history. As mentioned, most of Mexico's inhabitants professed local and regional rather than national allegiances. Indeed, a silver lining of the war with the United States might have been the fact that the conflict constituted a significant turning point in the emergence of a Mexican national consciousness. The lost war prompted a majority of propertied Mexicans to agree on a common front vis-à-vis the U.S. invasion force. They knew that Texas and all points west were lost forever, but they hoped to maintain the Mexican heartland under the authority of the federal government.

As a result, the Mexican elites broadly agreed on the need for some form of central government control. By the 1840s, the debate between Centralists and Federalists had shifted to one between the underlying political tendencies of both movements, Conservatism and Liberalism. For the most part, the Conservatives held many of the views of the former Centralists, and the

Liberals, many of those of the former Federalists, but there had been plenty of exceptions to this rule. The new conflict involved factions that were ideologically aligned to a greater extent than the Centralists and Federalists had been. Taking their cue from the progenitor of their movement, the statesman and historian Lucas Alamán, Conservatives clung to Catholic tradition, a social hierarchy, and limited engagement with the outside world. They desired to protect the socioeconomic order inherited from the colonial period and preserve the privileges of the Church and army. The Liberals, following the lead of two early Mexican Liberals, Valentín Gómez Farías and José María Luis Mora, desired to follow the example of the American and French revolutions in abolishing the fueros and all other special legal privileges, and they advocated democratic reforms to guarantee individual liberties. Unlike the Conservatives, the Liberals were split into two camps: the *puros*, or radical Liberals, who wanted to emulate the free-market capitalism and parliamentary democracy of the United States and to break the influence of the Church in order to bring Mexico into the modern world; and the *moderados*, or moderates, who feared popular uprisings and wished to retain the social hierarchy and some aspects of authoritarian rule.

REFORM, CIVIL WAR, AND FRENCH INTERVENTION, 1854–1867

All Liberals, whether puros or moderados, agreed on the definitive removal of Santa Anna from the politics of their nation. In 1854—just after Santa Anna had sold off a strip of Sonora to the United States in the Gadsden Purchase—they got their chance, as the long-time caudillo of the South, Juan Alvarez, joined their cause. On March 1, Colonel Florencio Villarreal proclaimed the Plan of Ayutla in the city of the same name in Guerrero. It not only proclaimed the intention to end the rule of Santa Anna once and for all, but also called for a constituent assembly to write a new constitution. A new generation of Liberal leaders supported the plan: among them were the creoles Ignacio Comonfort and Miguel Lerdo de Tejada, Melchor Ocampo, who had studied in Europe for many years, and the Zapotec Indian Benito Juárez. It took seventeen months for the Liberals to reach their goal. On August 8, 1855, Santa Anna resigned the presidency for the eleventh and final time, and Alvarez briefly became president before giving way to the moderado Comonfort.

Among the Liberal victors, none was more important than Benito Juárez. A Zapotec, Juárez was born in 1806 in the village of Guelatao, Oaxaca, into a poor family. He became an orphan as a three-year-old and worked as a shepherd at a very young age to sustain himself. At twelve years of age, he walked forty-one miles to the city of Oaxaca and began an apprenticeship as a printer. It was only then that Juárez learned Spanish, and he soon realized that the way up was through obtaining a formal education. After a brief stint studying in a seminary, Juárez studied law. Highly intelligent and articulate, he became the first attorney to receive official certification in the state of Oaxaca.

He began his political career at the age of twenty-six, when he was elected to the Oaxaca city council, but returned to the practice of law, where he distinguished himself in defending a village against its local priest. He became a man of means, which enabled him to marry a white woman, Margarita Maza, the daughter of Italian immigrants. He returned to politics, and in 1848 he won election as governor of his home state—the first indigenous Mexican ever elected to a governorship. During Santa Anna's last term in office, the caudillo had Juárez arrested and escorted to Veracruz, where the Oaxacan departed for exile in New Orleans. From Louisiana, Juárez plotted the overthrow of Santa Anna and secured Alvarez's support as well as the provision of arms and money to the rebels. Therefore, he played a crucial role in the victory of the Liberals in 1855.

Thus began the Liberal *Reforma*, a vast experiment to modernize Mexico along the lines of Great Britain and the United States. Even though the moderado Comonfort was president, it was puros such as Juárez and Lerdo de Tejada who took the lead in writing the most significant reform laws of the era. Juárez and Lerdo desired a capitalist, democratic, and secular nation in which individuals were equal before the law. In such a society, they believed, both the rich and the poor would compete for power on equal terms, free from the odious ethnic and professional distinctions created by the fueros, which allowed the clergy and members of the military to avoid trial in civil courts. The very first reform law, the Ley Juárez of 1855, restricted the fueros to violations of ecclesiastical and military law. The other reform laws entailed a direct attack on the Catholic Church. Authored by another puro Liberal, the Ley Lerdo barred what it labeled "corporations"—chiefly Church institutions and local governments—from owning land and real estate not essential to running their everyday operations. The law decreed that most of the vast landholdings of the Church would be auctioned off to private citizens. Liberals were not thinking, however, of providing landless campesinos with a plot to call their own; instead, they intended to foster private landownership in Mexico, with the lands going to the highest bidder. President Comonfort also approved a law giving the state—rather than the Church—the power to register births, marriages, and deaths. This law took away one of the principal sources of revenue of the Church. Finally, the new Constitution of 1857 codified these laws and created a parliamentary system in which the president would have to share power with a single legislature. Mexico, as the framers of this document believed, needed safeguards against dictatorship, and the Liberals hoped that the new document would prevent the emergence of a new strongman leader such as Santa Anna. The new constitution also omitted any mention of Catholicism as the state church, although it did not expressly safeguard freedom of religion, either. Neither the Church nor the Conservatives could accept this new state of things. From distant Rome, Pope Pius IX denounced the constitution. He and the Conservatives found help from the Mexican military, which—just like the Church—had lost important privileges through the reform laws. In 1858, General Félix Zuloaga pronounced himself in rebellion against Comonfort, jailed Juárez, the next in line for the presidency, and dissolved Congress.

Zuloaga's coup plunged Mexico into a most devastating civil war, the War of the Reform (1858–61). While the army proclaimed Zuloaga president, Juárez escaped to Querétaro, where he was named president by his Liberal allies as the first and only indigenous Mexican to occupy the country's highest office. The two national governments then went to war to determine national supremacy and the fate of the reform. The three-year war that ensued defied easy ideological or political categorization. For example, indigenous people fought on both sides of the conflict. Some of those who sided with the Liberals did so out of conviction that an open political system would provide them with more opportunities to express their grievances, and others admired Juárez. Other indigenous Mexicans such as the cacique Tomás Mejía supported the Conservatives because they feared that the Ley Lerdo might not just disentail the lands of the Church, but those of indigenous villages as well. Yet others followed the lead of the Conservative Party because they had been threatened or intimidated by the Church. Likewise, creoles and mestizos, city dwellers and country people, could be found on both sides of the conflict. After three years, the Liberals finally won a decisive defeat under General Ignacio Zaragoza. At the cost of tens of thousands of lives, it appeared that the advocates of reform had prevailed.

Yet a military victory such as this one could not breach the deep divide manifested by the Conservative-Liberal conflict—a divide that transcended the conflict between political factions dominated by the gente alta and decente to include the lower classes. The Liberal attack on the Church not only provoked the wrath of the Church hierarchy and other defenders of traditional privilege, but also the opposition of popular Catholicism. One example of the way traditional Catholics understood the conflict was through the cult of Madre Matiana, a sixteenth-century nun said to have been plagued by terrifying visions of a Satanic plot to throw the nation into turmoil by means of a constitution, an egalitarian legal code, and the establishment of legislative rule. According to nineteenth-century Catholic pamphlets, Matiana prophesied the incursion of U.S. armies, civil war, and the expropriation of Church property. These pamphlets ascribed to Matiana the role of a visionary who anticipated the chaos and violence of nineteenth-century Mexico. On the other side of the debate, the Liberals viewed the Catholic Church as the primary obstacle toward the establishment of a capitalist and democratic society like the United States. Popular liberalism also viewed the Church as a foreign-controlled institution that purposefully kept millions of Mexicans in ignorance and poverty. Liberals believed the Church to be the last holdover of Spanish rule, an institution that kept Mexico repeating colonial patterns.

Hopes for peace thus proved ephemeral. The Liberals bickered over the treatment of their enemies, and President Juárez confronted a Congress that took its charge to check executive power seriously. Mexico was also in a deep financial crisis. Due to the war, the government had not paid its civil servants or police for three years. The country's infrastructure lagged decades behind that of many other Latin American countries. While investors in the United States strung together a network of railroads that soon connected the Atlantic to the Pacific coasts, not a single serviceable railroad line existed in Mexico that linked two major cities. A typical journey from Mexico City to Veracruz took at least three days, and several weeks in the rainy season. The government was also deeply in debt to its creditors from France, Great Britain, and Spain and besieged by claims from private citizens from these nations who had suffered losses during the War of Reform. On October 31, 1861, delegates from the creditor nations agreed to collect on these debts in the Convention of London. The terms of the agreement stipulated the occupation by forces of the three signatory powers of both coasts and forced debt collection by means of seizing the customs house of Veracruz. But the French Emperor Napoleon III had even more ambitious plans. He desired to establish a virtual French colony in the Americas. When the British and Spanish officers in Veracruz realized the scope of these ambitions, they sent their troops home; their departure left Napoleon's troops alone to carry out their leader's grandiose plans for conquest.

Less than a month after Queen Victoria of England and Queen Isabella II of Spain withdrew their forces from the Mexican coasts, more than six thousand French troops marched inland. Aware of the success of General Scott's army just sixteen years before, the French did not expect much resistance, and they were encouraged by the fact that both the Conservatives and the Church supported the invasion. But on May 5, 1862, Zaragoza's soldiers defeated the invaders in the Battle of Puebla, a victory still celebrated each year during the Cinco de Mayo festivities. Among the Mexican officers distinguishing themselves in the battle was a young mestizo from Oaxaca, Brigadier General Porfirio Díaz, who would become Mexico's longest-serving ruler later in the century. But the Mexican triumph was short-lived. Aided by more than thirty thousand reinforcements, the French regrouped and laid siege to Puebla in March 1863. The city fell after two months, and in late May, Juárez gave up Mexico City without a fight. While Juárez and his cabinet evacuated to San Luis Potosí, the French seized the capital and named a provisional government consisting of thirty-five Conservative notables, including several former allies of Santa Anna. The French had found domestic allies to support their occupation and hunkered down for what they believed would be a long-term presence in Mexico.

But this was only an intermediate step to Napoleon's larger goal: the naming of a European monarch as Emperor of Mexico, a monarch who would rule by the force of French arms. He found his man in Archduke Ferdinand Maximilian of Austria, the younger brother of Emperor Franz Joseph I. Maximilian readily assented provided that a plebiscite would validate his reign. This condition indicated that the future emperor would not always do the bidding of his Conservative and French backers. Although the plebiscite administered by the French army confirmed Maximilian in his new office, he had served notice that he, like Juárez and the other Liberals, valued the principle of popular sovereignty. But he also knew who his master was. In the Convention of Miramar, Maximilian accepted the throne and promised to reimburse Napoleon for the costs of the military occupation, including the wages of the French troops while in Mexico. He also guaranteed the payment of all French claims in full.

In late May 1864, Maximilian and his wife Charlotte (known to Mexicans as Carlota) arrived in Veracruz aboard an Austrian vessel. They brought with them all the accouterments of a European court: furniture, china, servants, cooks, bureaucrats, and even two ladies-in-waiting. Hot and humid Veracruz, however, offered a rude awakening to the realities of a very different region of the world from the one Maximilian and Carlota had left. Upon viewing the dilapidated port facilities, the royal couple realized the enormous task of achieving economic development in a country that had seen more than half a century of political unrest and economic stagnation. In Mexico, yellow fever plagued the coast, striking down thousands of people each year. Black vultures hovered over the town, ready to pick at moldering carcasses in the streets. The welcome party sent to greet the monarchs arrived late, and the journey to Mexico City took several days. The railroad ended in a tiny village in the Sierra Madre, whence stagecoaches brought the royal party to the capital. Once there, the couple felt more at home, as the cool mountain air of Mexico City was much more to their liking. Maximilian and Carlota installed themselves in lofty Chapultepec Castle, the residence of Mexican presidents.

Maximilian's rule contributed to the growth of foreign cultural influence. The French brought their cuisine to Mexico, and the Austrians their pastry. French thought already molded the worldview of the elite in Mexico City, and the French and Austrian presence gave further impetus to those ideas. The Austrian polka left its imprint in the waltz rhythms and brass instrumentation of *ranchera* music, and French soldiers left their genetic imprint in the provinces such as Los Altos, Jalisco, in the form of their children from mixed unions. But just as the new emperor advanced the Europeanization of Mexico, so did Maximilian endeavor to make himself Mexican. Upon entering Mexico City, he made his first stop at the Basílica de Guadalupe, a gesture designed to appeal to both the Church and the indigenous and mestizo majority. Maximilian also opened his palace to the public once a week; he spent a lot of time wandering around in marketplaces; he ate Mexican food; and he sometimes even wore indigenous garments. According to French military officer Charles Blanchot, Maximilian visited indigenous communities in order to relieve a tortured soul that was taxed beyond its limits by the task of governing Mexico: "When his state of irritation became too acute, and when the burden of his job seemed too heavy, His Majesty would go on a little trip. Amidst the ovations of the poor, morose Indians, he found relief and pleasure, as he considered himself adored by his subjects."

While the blond and blue-eyed Maximilian's efforts to Mexicanize himself produced bemusement among both the French occupation army and the Mexico City elite, his policies engendered controversy. To the consternation of his Conservative allies, Maximilian issued a series of decrees reminiscent of Liberal policies. Assisted by Mexican advisers steeped in modern French thought, a group dubbed *los imperialistas*, he decreed freedom of the press and the abolition of debt peonage. The new emperor did not treat the Church much differently than had Juárez. He refused to reinstate lands lost during the Reforma, and he even imposed several forced loans on the Church. A Freemason, Maximilian held views more in line with those of the Liberals than those of the Conservatives. The Liberals, however, refused to come to terms with the emperor. From their point of view, Maximilian was a usurper, a foreign ruler imposed by an army of occupation. Driven back all the way to the U.S. border near El Paso, Texas, Juárez and his allies realized that a Mexican Empire was not viable in the long run and drew nationalist credentials from their rejection of Maximilian and the French occupation. They knew that U.S. President Abraham Lincoln could not but reject Maximilian on the grounds of the Monroe Doctrine, which denounced the establishment of new European colonies in the Americas. In 1865, the victory of the Union over the Confederacy in the U.S. Civil War assured Juárez of U.S. military support, as Lincoln wasted no time pressuring Napoleon to withdraw his forces from Mexico. Tired of an occupation that had become increasingly expensive and ineffective, Napoleon began to remove French soldiers in late 1866 and early 1867. The Lincoln administration also allowed the Juaristas to purchase arms in the United States.

In the end, these three factors—Liberal nationalism, the position of the United States, and the French withdrawal—doomed Maximilian's empire. In the spring of 1866, the Juaristas seized the offensive and occupied the strategic northern cities of Chihuahua, Monterrey, and Matamoros. During the remainder of the year, the Liberals seized the rest of the north as well as Guadalajara and Oaxaca and encircled Maximilian in central Mexico. The end came in June 1867, when the Juaristas captured Maximilian in the city of Querétaro. Mindful of the fact that the emperor had ordered the execution of all captured Liberal commanders at the height of his power in 1865, Juárez had Maximilian court-martialed and sentenced to death. On the morning of June 19, 1867, a firing squad executed Maximilian and some of his closest Mexican allies on a hill outside Querétaro.

The executions sent a message that Mexico was a sovereign nation, but they also served up an eerie reminder that being a Mexican head of state was a hazardous profession. Sovereignty had come at a terrible price: at least 50,000 casualties in the last war alone, decades of political strife, economic crisis, and foreign intervention accompanied by the loss of half of the country's territory. But this hard-won sovereignty had only heightened the sense that Mexico needed a strong central government and a series of reforms to survive. It fell to Juárez and his allies to oversee the resulting process of Liberal modernization intended to make Mexico, at last, a nation equal to the invaders that had plagued its first decades of existence as an independent country.

CHAPTER THREE

❧ Liberal Modernization ☙

*R*eyes Domínguez embodied law and order in the mountain village of Tomochic, Chihuahua. Most of the three hundred largely mestizo inhabitants
of this drought-stricken hamlet knew him as the "village son of a bitch."
The cacique owned most of the surrounding land, much of it too parched to
be of use; he controlled access to water; and through bribes and threats, he
dominated local officials as well. His political connections reached up to the
Terrazas clan, a family whose land holdings equaled the size of the U.S. state of
South Carolina, and to President Porfirio Díaz. He was but one of thousands
of caciques across all of Mexico who subscribed to the nineteenth-century
notion of "order and progress." Order meant the rule of law, and, if necessary,
repression. Progress was a code word for European, and specifically French,
culture, and caciques like Reyes Domínguez dreamed of a future in which
Mexico shared the prosperity and material advancements of the European
nation that had invaded it just a few decades before.

But Reyes Domínguez did not own the hearts and minds of the residents
of Tomochic. That role fell to his brother-in-law, Cruz Chávez, the village's
spiritual leader. Chávez and his followers believed that justice came only by
the grace of God. They chafed under official restrictions of popular religion,
and especially the prohibition of unauthorized religious pilgrimages. In 1891, a
visiting minister threatened to close down church services that he deemed too
unorthodox, and Chávez and his followers left Tomochic for the local religious
site of El Chopeque. Along the way, the group met a detachment of *rurales*,
Díaz's rural police infamous for their brutality. The encounter resulted in the
death of one of Chávez's men. Incited by a nearby faith healer, Teresa Urrea,
also known as "la Santa de Caborca," the people of Tomochic and surround-

ing areas erupted in rebellion. When Teresa railed against "priests, money, and doctors," she questioned the very material progress that formed the bedrock of Reyes Domínguez's worldview. The challenge to Liberal modernization would not go unanswered. When a local indigenous revolt invoked Teresa's name, President Díaz exiled her to Arizona, and in October 1892, government forces wiped out the rebels. Progress, Díaz believed, had triumphed, and Mexico at long last had a government that could make its decisions respected in remote corners of the republic. But the incident lived on in popular memory, and rural Chihuahuans awaited the day that would bring redemption.

The Tomochic rebellion illustrates the contradictions of the era of Liberal modernization (1867–1911). At long last free of their Conservative rivals, the Liberals took advantage of the rapid expansion of the North Atlantic economies to attract investment capital to Mexico and centralize political power. Initially, parliamentary rule prevailed in the Restored Republic (1867–76) under Presidents Juárez and Sebastián Lerdo de Tejada. In 1876, General Porfirio Díaz seized power in a military coup. Díaz dominated the political landscape for the next thirty-five years and served as president for thirty-one years, most of them as dictator. Hence historians know this long period from 1876 to 1911 as the Porfiriato, the longest period of one-man rule Mexico has ever seen. Under Díaz, order and progress became a political recipe that—as the people of Tomochic experienced firsthand—brought progress for some and repression to others.

THE ELEMENTS OF MODERNIZATION, 1867–1890

When Juárez returned to the presidency in July 1867, he found himself at the helm of a country that was in even worse shape than before the Liberal triumph in 1854. The Restored Republic had at last brought parliamentary rule, but the national government had no money and enjoyed little authority outside Mexico City. Infrastructure and communications remained poor, allowing regional caudillos to maintain the independent spheres of power that their predecessors had carved out during and after the independence wars. Bad roads, internal tariffs, and rampant crime hampered overland trade; it could take three weeks or more to reach Mexico City from the coast. Only two hundred miles of railroad track existed, most of it between the capital and Veracruz. But not even that crucial route had been completed, and stagecoaches and mules transported goods and passengers over a fifty-mile stretch in the Sierra Madre Oriental. Half a century after the Wars of Independence, most of the silver mines had still not resumed production, and von Humboldt's 1803 visit had marked the last effort of note to find new ore. Likewise, agriculture remained in an eighteenth-century state, without the use of fertilizers or machinery. Mexico's cities and towns had grown greatly in size due to the influx of migrants fleeing war and devastation in the countryside, without providing enough jobs for the newcomers.

A survivor of hard-fought wars, Juárez found that being the elected ruler of a nation destroyed by decades of civil war and foreign intervention required adapting his Liberal ideas to these harsh realities. He was no longer the idealistic reformer he had been in the 1850s. After Juárez defeated Porfirio Díaz in the 1867 presidential elections, he increasingly turned to authoritarian methods. He rigged state and local elections to get his favorites into power, and Díaz alleged that the presidential elections had been marred by fraud as well. Juárez also attempted to amend the constitution to curtail the rights of Congress and the states guaranteed in the Constitution of 1857. The president confronted a budget shortage even greater than the one he had faced in the 1850s. As a result, he pared down the army from 60,000 to 20,000 men, dismissing the remainder without the benefit of a government pension. In search of sustenance, many of these former troops returned to their home towns, often still in possession of the firearms issued to them by the government. Once there, many of them enforced the law in their own name as bandits.

Juárez confronted this upsurge in banditry by means of a new military unit, the rurales. The legislation authorizing the rurales came from the 1850s, but it was not until ten years later that Congress earmarked sufficient funding for them. The rurales were heavily armed military guards on horseback, many of them commissioned from among bandits willing to ply their trade in the employ of the government. As enforcers of law and order who answered only to the federal Secretariat of the Interior, the rurales eluded the checks and balances of the parliamentary system that the Liberals had created. The formation of the rurales was but one piece of evidence of the Liberals' shift away from the safeguarding of individual liberties, and toward an authoritarian concept of rule.

Another piece of evidence of such a shift was the emergence of a technocratic governing elite. This oligarchy resembled the imperialistas that had surrounded Emperor Maximilian in that they were trained in French thought and considered themselves the harbingers of modernization. One of the differences between them and the imperialistas was that the new technocrats were anticlerical. The protagonist of this group was Gabino Barreda, Juárez's secretary of justice and founder of the Escuela Nacional Preparatoria (ENP, or National Preparatory School). In the mold of the French philosopher Auguste

Comte, Barreda was a positivist, someone who believed that all problems had a scientific and rationally ascertainable solution. Barreda was committed to building up a national education system in a country that lacked basic secondary education everywhere but in larger towns and cities. The ENP followed a positivist curriculum that included rigorous instruction in math, science, and logic, but little training in the arts and humanities, and it taught its almost exclusively creole students to think of themselves as the intellectual elite of the nation. Barreda envisioned public education as serving the needs of the Liberal nation-state by molding productive and loyal citizens. In his famous "Oración cívica" (Civic Oration) of 1867, Barreda proposed the "mental emancipation" of the Mexican people from what he viewed as Catholic superstition and localist narrowness of vision. He believed that Juárez's triumph had brought a time of "liberty, order, and progress" to Mexico, and that it was up to the government to instill in all citizens a "scientific" approach to both public administration and private life. These views encapsulated the doctrine of scientific politics, the notion that technocrats, rather than politicians, should shape a nation's destiny. Popular among the white elites throughout the Atlantic world, this worldview heralded a convergence of the Conservative ideal of order with the Liberal quest for progress. According to the historian Charles Hale, classical liberalism, concerned with individual liberties and democracy, transformed itself at this time into positivism, which emphasized economic development and the building of a strong, authoritarian central state. Indeed, "order and progress" became the motto of Latin American modernizers in the last third of the nineteenth century, and to this day the phrase is shown draped around the globe on the Brazilian national flag.

The ruling Liberals therefore remained consistent in their laissez-faire economic policies. A former Mexican minister in Paris, Juárez knew that the Industrial Revolution was transforming North America and western Europe at the very time that Mexicans fought one war after another. For the Liberals, the most significant condition of modernization in material terms was the building of railroads. Therefore, the opening of this last segment in a mountainous landscape in 1872 was cause for celebration. Still, a far more ambitious project lay ahead: to connect central Mexico with the U.S. border as a way to facilitate the export of agricultural and mineral resources, and as a means of effectively bringing the vast and underpopulated north under central political control. Juárez did not live to see that feat, as he died of a heart attack on July 19, 1872. In accordance with the constitution, Sebastián Lerdo de Tejada, the brother of Miguel and the president of the Supreme Court, succeeded him in office. Beginning in October 1872, Lerdo won and served a full four-year term as president, the first time in Mexican history that two consecutive presidential administrations had not been overthrown by violence.

The creole Lerdo brought a different style of rule. A polished and well-educated orator, the new president quickly won the admiration of the urban elite, but he disdained rural Mexico and the indigenous and mestizo majority. To a far greater extent than Juárez, Lerdo believed in centralist rule, and he resented the political conflict and debate that forms an important part of democracy. As he put it, Mexico needed "less politics and more administration." Thus Lerdo strengthened the rurales and other parts of the political machine his predecessor had begun to build. Under his watch, southeastern Mexico witnessed a boom in tropical export commodities such as rubber, coffee, and cocoa, and Lerdo planned to foster this boom by improving the railroad system, particularly by means of a line traversing the Isthmus of Tehuantepec. He was more cautious regarding railroad lines to the U.S. border, and he reportedly once remarked: "Between weakness and strength, let there be the desert!" Lerdo also improved the country's education system, doubling the number of students enrolled in primary and secondary schools. Under the leadership of graduates from Barreda's ENP, the college preparatory and university education in Mexico City greatly improved. To be sure, education in the nation as a whole was another matter. In 1874, almost 95 percent of school-age children did not attend school, and most of them could not read and write. In most states, students could not pursue an education past the ninth grade, and obtaining the equivalent of a high school diploma meant relocating to a large city like Mexico City or Guadalajara. Nonetheless, Lerdo's tenure as president had been successful enough that he decided to run for another term in 1876.

Once again, however, General Porfirio Díaz challenged him. Díaz enjoyed considerable support as one of the best military leaders the Liberals had. Like Juárez, he hailed from Oaxaca, where he was born in the state capital in 1830 to an indigenous mother and a mestizo father who died when Porfirio was three years old. And like his fellow Oaxacan, Díaz grew up poor, albeit as a Spanish speaker, and sought upward social mobility in a seminary and a stint at the State Institute for Arts and Sciences, where Juárez had studied law decades earlier. Unlike Juárez, however, Díaz came of age at the heyday of foreign intervention and civil war in the late 1840s and 1850s, a context that explains his decision to join the army rather than the legal profession in his quest for greater opportunities. He joined the Liberals at the time of the Ayutla revolt and obtained his first military rank during the War of Reform.

He was a hero of Cinco de Mayo, 1862, and Díaz and his forces took Mexico City from Maximilian in 1867.

Thus Porfirio Díaz believed that the presidency should be his. Twice he ran unsuccessfully for president against Juárez (in 1867 and 1871), and on two other occasions, he attempted to overthrow the government by force. In the winter of 1876, afraid that the army would thwart yet another of his attempted coups, Díaz approached U.S. investors with a plea for their support. He bitterly complained that Lerdo was afraid of the United States—so afraid of an invasion, Díaz claimed, that the president had refused to build railroads all the way to the border. Pledging himself to build these railroads, Díaz won the financial support of numerous entrepreneurs from South Texas. With the help of their funds, Díaz staged yet another coup in November 1876, this time under the Plan of Tuxtepec. Demanding "effective suffrage, no reelection," the plan alleged that Lerdo had resorted to widespread electoral fraud, and it criticized the president for seeking another term despite the existence of a provision in the constitution that forbade reelection. This time, Díaz was successful and finally won what he thought had been his right since his heroism on Cinco de Mayo: the presidency of Mexico.

Initially, however, the Porfirian regime needed to fight for its survival. After his successful coup, Díaz faced a standoff with U.S. President Ulysses S. Grant, who withheld diplomatic recognition of his regime as a point of leverage to obtain concessions in a number of border and financial disputes. Having failed in this endeavor, Grant left the situation to his successor, Rutherford B. Hayes, who had himself come to power in a highly disputed election. Eager to disguise his own lack of a popular mandate, Hayes dispatched troops to the border under General Edward Ord. For his part, Díaz ordered General Gerónimo Treviño to resist a possible invasion. At the height of this crisis, Díaz found the help of the very U.S. railroad and industrial magnates who had funded the Tuxtepec Rebellion. In April 1878, Hayes awarded Mexico under Díaz diplomatic recognition and withdrew U.S. forces from the border. Soon thereafter, Treviño married Ord's daughter, highlighting the symbolic end of animosities.

This incident showed Díaz that foreign investors could be better allies than foreign governments. As relations with the United States remained volatile, Díaz increasingly relied on foreign investors to smooth out differences with the powerful "northern colossus." In this effort, he was able to count on growing demand for Mexican export products, as western Europe and the United States rapidly industrialized in the last three decades of the nineteenth century. Industrialization created demand for tropical export commodities such as coffee, rubber, and sugar, as well as mining products such as copper and silver. Mexico came to play a crucial role in an expanding Atlantic economy that traded Latin American raw materials for U.S. and European finished products.

In 1880, Díaz stepped aside in favor of a protégé, Manuel González, honoring his promise to relinquish power after one presidential term. A four-year interlude in what was otherwise a thirty-five year period dominated by Porfirio Díaz, the González presidency witnessed many of the most important legal reforms that would facilitate the modernization of Mexico. As a network of railroads financed by British and U.S. capital began to connect Mexico and the United States, González promised foreign businesses generous concessions. During his rule, the Mexican Congress passed a slew of legislation amending the old colonial-era Spanish agricultural and mining codes to fit the mold of Anglo American capitalism. The old Spanish laws had considered the land and subsoil the patrimony of the Mexican nation, and they had made an express distinction between ownership of land (which could be either public or private) and ownership of the mineral resources of the subsoil, which was vested in the nation alone. These laws largely protected the land of indigenous villages and made the private purchase of land expensive and cumbersome. Moreover, Mexican and foreign investors could only act as concessionaires rather than owners of mining enterprises, and they had to pay high taxes for the extraction of mineral resources. The most important of the new laws was the so-called "Baldíos Law" of 1883, which allowed the government to seize land it considered fallow, or unused, and to sell it to private investors. The crux was, of course, that any agribusiness could seek to have land declared fallow, and that bribery of public officials opened the door for misappropriation of land, particularly that of small landowners and indigenous communities. The Baldíos Law provided another tool to those who could pay to get the decisions they wanted from courts and officials. Thus, González did the dirty work for don Porfirio—the construction of a legal framework that aided the formation of large private estates at the expense of the poor majority. Another law allowed both domestic and foreign proprietors to exploit freely the subsoil underneath their land.

After Díaz's return to power in 1884, a power he would not relinquish until 1911, Mexican foreign policy sought to balance the desires of foreign investors against those of Mexican nationalists. Two experienced advisers helped Díaz with this balancing act: the Secretary of Foreign Relations, Ignacio Mariscal, and Matías Romero, the chief Mexican diplomatic representative in the United States. Even though both of these former associates of Juárez hailed from the state of Oaxaca, they held widely different views. Despite his marriage to a North American woman, the nationalist Mariscal, who remained close to military circles, held a profound mistrust of U.S. intentions and advocated stronger efforts to attract European capital. The pro-business Romero, on the other hand, regarded the United States as the main potential source of the capital needed to build up Mexico's infrastructure. Whereas Mariscal feared that the flow of U.S. investments might one day amount to a "Pacific Conquest" no less dangerous than the U.S.–Mexican War, Romero thought that the existence of strong economic links would make U.S. aggression much less likely. Díaz used the advice of both politicians to construct his foreign policy: Mariscal shaped inter-American and European diplomacy, and Romero handled most of the negotiations with U.S. investors from his office in Washington.

Material progress, however, was slow to arrive, and mindsets even harder to change. After visiting Mexico City in 1884, the Anglo-French journalist Clément Bertie-Marriott ridiculed the nation's inhabitants for grafting French food and customs onto what he viewed as a rural and backward society. He also criticized bullfighting—since Spanish colonial rule one of the country's most popular pastimes—as a barbaric sport. The U.S. visitor Fanny Chambers Gooch expressed herself in even less charitable terms concerning the inhabitants of the rural north, alleging that Mexicans were too lazy and superstitious to take advantage of the blessings of modern technology. Ever mindful of foreign opinion, the gente alta heeded critiques such as these, and the government temporarily banned bullfights from Mexico City. Instead, it promoted "modern" sports such as bicycling.

Thus the Porfiriato witnessed the triumph of the positivist ideology Barreda had pioneered a few decades earlier: order and progress. This belief included admiration for foreign ways, particularly French culture and U.S. technology, but also a sense that Mexico could make a unique contribution to the emerging cosmopolitan world. As Bertie-Marriott had sensed correctly, the elite of Mexico City measured itself by French standards yet knew they fell short in that regard. Over the next twenty years, the Porfirians transformed themselves and their country. Díaz himself was perhaps the most obvious harbinger of change. In 1881, at 51 years of age, the recently widowed leader married his 17-year-old English tutor. His new wife was Carmen Romero Rubio, the daughter of a famous creole family from Mexico City that had numbered among Lerdo's staunchest supporters. The marriage to doña Carmelita, as most Mexicans came to know her, was a great political triumph for Díaz, as the family relationship allowed Díaz to mend relations with his enemies within the Liberal movement. It was a good example of the significance of clientelism in Mexican politics. Doña Carmelita helped transform the mestizo Díaz into a polished gentleman. Over time, French military garb and liberal amounts of facial powder gave Díaz the appearance of a French general.

For his part, Manuel Romero Rubio, Díaz's new father-in-law who was only two years older than don Porfirio, became the founding father of the *científicos*, a circle of positivist advisers that would rise to great political and financial importance in the Porfirian regime. Most of Romero Rubio's young associates in this circle were graduates of the ENP, convinced that politics was a matter of practical and scientific application. The leading científico newspaper, *La Libertad*, was an important propaganda instrument for the Díaz regime, arguing that Mexicans needed a strong hand rather than the chaos of democracy. The científico editorials in *La Libertad* recommended that Mexicans follow the guidance of their nation's best-trained minds, those who considered themselves the most fit to steer the destiny of the country. The científico ascendancy completed the transformation of the ruling Liberals from idealists advocating human rights and democracy to supporters of an authoritarian regime. Those Liberals who disagreed found themselves on the outside of the ruling circle. Among the members of the científicos were the Finance Minister, José Yves Limantour, the Undersecretary of Public Instruction, Justo Sierra, and many other members of the Díaz cabinet.

Despite their common background, the científicos were by no means uniform in their thinking. In particular, they disagreed about the place of Mexico's indigenous and mestizo majority in the future of the nation. Some of them were adherents of Herbert Spencer's social Darwinism, which applied Darwin's theories of natural history to the human social order. In the late nineteenth century, when European powers carved up most of the globe in colonial empires, "survival of the fittest" was used to justify the rule of well-educated white people just like the científicos themselves. The social Darwinists among the group argued that indigenous people had no useful role to play in society beyond providing menial labor. They believed that progress could only come through the "whitening" of Mexico by large-scale European immigration of the kind that transformed Argentina, Brazil, Canada, and the United States at the turn of the century. Other científicos were Comte-style positivists like their mentor, Barreda, and believed that people of color were just as educable as were Europeans. Justo Sierra, for instance, favored the expansion of public education in order to bring the "Indian" into the Mexican nation as a productive citizen, and he envisioned an amalgamated nation in which ethnicity and race no longer mattered.

The power held by the científico group again affirmed the significance of clientelist connections. Membership among the científicos opened doors to both political power and prosperity in Porfirian Mexico. The científicos enjoyed close ties to both foreign investors and local power brokers, who served as their connection to local and regional politics. Over time, these clientelist relationships became a virtual prerequisite for partaking in the Porfirian spoils system.

THE REWARDS OF MODERNIZATION, 1890–1900

By any standard, the Porfiriato brought impressive material improvements to Mexico. For example, Díaz's long rule witnessed the construction of almost 15,000 miles of railroad track. Because of the mountains, the lines ran mainly in a north-south direction. U.S. and British investors owned most of the new railroad lines, and the majority of the track connected the major cities and export-producing regions to the U.S. border. This venture had momentous consequences for the Mexican north, hitherto a sparsely populated region. The railroad facilitated both economic development and the assertion of central political authority in the region. For example, the coming of the railroad facilitated the development of copper mining in Sonora, cattle ranching in Chihuahua, and cotton growing in Coahuila. Political centralization accompanied economic development, as regional elites had to reckon with the fact that the railroad could bring federal troops to a distant region within twenty-four hours. The railroad therefore provided a major boost to the Porfirian aim of political centralization.

The revival of the mining industry was an equally impressive achievement. Since independence, Mexican silver mining had played only a negligible role in the economy. Until Manuel González's term, the nation held theoretical ownership of subsoil resources, a principal obstacle to the development of this sector by private businesses. As mentioned, in 1884, new legislation allowed a landowner free exploitation of the resources underneath it, and shortly thereafter, the Porfirians drastically lowered tax rates on mining products. Moreover, state-of-the-art technology facilitated unprecedented levels of silver production at new sites such as Sierra Mojada, Coahuila, and Batopilas, Chihuahua. Not adjusted for inflation, silver production figures grew from 1.5

to 40 million pesos between 1877 and 1908, surpassing in real terms the levels of the late colony. Copper production witnessed an even more spectacular rise during the Porfirian period.

The surge in Mexican silver production had momentous consequences for the world economy. In an era when the coinage of precious metals still constituted the most significant source of new capital, the production of millions of new silver pesos capitalized markets as far away as China and India. Throughout most of Asia, the "Mexican dollar" was accepted as legal tender. The downside of this phenomenon was that the pesos flooded financial markets, putting pressure on world silver prices. Twice during the Porfiriato—in 1893 and 1905—a precipitous decline in the price of silver wreaked havoc with the Mexican economy. In the long term, the overproduction of silver devalued the peso and increased the cost of foreign-produced goods priced in dollars and English pounds, currencies backed by gold. In turn, the growing disparity in the purchasing power of the silver-denominated peso and the gold-denominated foreign currencies increased the earnings gap in companies where foreigners and Mexicans worked side by side. While foreign workers paid in dollars found their wages stable in real terms, Mexicans paid in pesos suffered a decline in real wages in the early 1900s.

The Porfirian era also saw the beginning of Mexican industrialization. One engine for this process was the development of an oil industry under the leadership of U.S. oil magnate Edward Doheny and his British counterpart, Weetman Pearson (later Sir Cowdray). The availability of domestic oil and coal allowed the emergence of Mexico's first steel foundry, the "Fundidora de Fierro y Acero de Monterrey." Located in the northern city of Monterrey, the Fundidora was the largest steel mill in all of Latin America, and it helped inaugurate the growth of what would soon be Mexico's preeminent industrial city. Monterrey also became the home of a brewery and a glass factory. Another industrial center emerged near the city of Orizaba, Puebla, the site of textile production and another brewery. Although industrialization did not achieve the central importance in turn-of-the-century Mexico that it had attained in the United States and western Europe, it was nonetheless noteworthy, for it contributed to the growth of an urban middle class. Industrial development encouraged more inhabitants to move to the cities, and it created a demand for professionals such as teachers, doctors, and lawyers, as well as white-collar employees in the industries themselves. Perhaps more than any other social group, this new middle class was the main beneficiary of Porfirian economic growth. For that reason, this group was also particularly vulnerable and liable to protest if its newfound significance appeared at risk.

The industrialization of Mexico created a powerful new group within the governing elite. Led by General Bernardo Reyes, a native of Monterrey who enjoyed close ties to the city's new industrial bourgeoisie, a rival faction came to challenge the científicos. For example, Foreign Secretary Ignacio Mariscal—though himself neither a military man nor an industrialist—also associated with this faction. Common to this group was their aversion of the científicos, whom they regarded as a cosmopolitan intelligentsia that had lost the connection to their home country. Mariscal's group was concerned about the degree to which foreign investors had obtained exclusive concessions in Mexico, and they resented the fact that many científicos had benefited personally from the awarding of these concessions. Until his death in 1910, Mariscal advocated nationalist policies designed to keep these concessions to a minimum and oppose U.S. efforts to gain more influence throughout Latin America. In this regard, the War of 1898, which pitted the United States against Spain in a conflict about the future of the Spanish colonial empire that still included Cuba, the Philippines, and Puerto Rico, marked a watershed in the relationship between these two groups. While the científicos regarded the war as unimportant for Mexico, Mariscal's faction was concerned about the growth of U.S. power in the Caribbean. In the end, Mexico remained neutral in the conflict, and upon Mariscal's urging, Mexico only recognized the independence of Cuba once the United States had won the war.

Porfirian modernization also led to an unprecedented degree of foreign influence in the economy. By 1910, nationals and corporations from France, Germany, Great Britain, Spain, and the United States had carved out spheres of influence in the Mexican economy. The French established the nation's first department stores, and they controlled large finance and industrial textile production. The Germans dominated the sale of hardware and kitchen items, and they owned numerous coffee plantations in the state of Chiapas. The British owned many of the mines, and Sir Cowdray held the country's largest oil concession. The Spaniards remained influential in retail commerce, and Spanish farmers controlled many of the tobacco plantations in Oaxaca and Veracruz. Finally, U.S. entrepreneurs came to constitute the single most influential group of investors. Historian John M. Hart has estimated that U.S. farmers and corporations owned no less than 10 percent of all arable land in Mexico in 1910. The Guggenheims and other magnates held a commanding stake in copper production, and Standard Oil of New Jersey was one of the big players in oil production. Most of the rubber plantations in the gulf state of Tabasco were owned by U.S. citizens, and the International Harvester Company controlled the processing and distribution in Yucatán of henequen, a product of the agave plant used to make twine for binding the North American wheat crop. A similar growth of foreign influence occurred in the rest of Latin America. In fact, the Southern Cone (an area that comprises Argentina, Chile, southern Brazil, and Uruguay) witnessed a far more drastic transformation through the arrival of millions of European immigrants. By contrast, Mexico, which lacked the extensive tracts of arable land found in the Southern Cone, received only a smattering of immigrants, most of them well-to-do.

Given this increasing foreign influence in Mexico—an influence that was cultural as well as economic and political—it was not surprising that the Porfiriato ushered in lifestyle patterns borrowed from France and the United States. By 1900, Mexico City boasted a modern post office, electrical lighting in the entire downtown district, and even department stores, the latest and clearest sign yet that the world was about to enter into what would later be dubbed the "American century." Department stores had originated in the 1870s and 1880s in Paris, London, Chicago, and New York City, where establishments such as "Macy's" remain famous to this day. The first Mexican department store was "El Palacio de Hierro" (The Iron Palace), a store built by the Tron family of France. The Palacio de Hierro was particularly famous for its clothes; it imported the latest fashions from Paris, but it also revolutionized Mexican manufacturing by making and selling relatively inexpensive undergarments made in Mexican sweat shops according to the specifications of French tailors. Thus the Trons marketed French fashion in Mexico, but also spearheaded the Mexican textile industry in Orizaba. Another large store was the "Casa Boker," designed in 1900 by U.S. architects for a German immigrant family. The Casa Boker was one of Mexico City's leading hardware stores, selling tools, kitchenware, carriages, and even insurance. Like the Palacio de Hierro, the Casa Boker primarily sold imported merchandise, but its catalog also included the heavy iron and steel products of the Fundidora de Fierro y Acero.

Yet the capital was a show case of the flip side of modernization as well. A few blocks east of the department stores began another city: a city populated by the léperos. For the inhabitants of eastern Mexico City, as well as in much of the rest of the nation, shopping trips to the Palacio de Hierro were unthinkable. Their ranks included beggars and workers who survived on centavos a day, servants or employees who left their jobs in the posh department store district every night for a world without electricity, safe drinking water, or sewers. Theirs was a dangerous world in which crime and poor sanitary conditions took the lives of many people before their time, yet it was a part of Mexico that the rich neither frequented nor cared to understand.

The rich had many weapons at their disposal to oppress the poor majority. For example, they controlled the interpretation of the law. The vagrancy laws, for instance, became one of the most important instruments to extort free labor from the less fortunate. In theory, the vagrancy laws were directed against homeless people loitering in public spaces, and they gave municipal authorities the right to arrest vagrants and compel them to work for the public good. In practice, a landowner in need of workers to pave his courtyard could bribe the mayor to invoke the vagrancy laws against the city's poor inhabitants. Without recourse to due process of law, these laborers were convicted on fabricated charges and sentenced to do free work for the landowner. Even more egregious was the abuse of the Baldíos Law. On paper, the law made fallow and unoccupied land, as mentioned, subject to expropriation and sale by the federal government. In reality, an investor interested in a piece of rural real estate could pay off a local official to have land of indigenous villages declared "fallow" even though the inhabitants cultivated it each and every year. None of these schemes to make a mockery of the law were new, but during the Porfiriato, the wealthy used these tools to assert their power to an unprecedented extent.

THE SEEDS OF DISCONTENT, 1900–1910

The first decade of the twentieth century witnessed the gradual unraveling of the Porfiriato. The causes for this crisis were diverse. In the first place, Díaz became more repressive as he aged, and he refused to groom a successor even though he had turned seventy in 1900. Also, a severe worldwide economic downturn hit Mexico in 1906–07, once again depressing the prices of exports as well as real wages. But perhaps the greatest reason for the disintegration of the Porfiriato lay in the uneven effect of modernization. Entrepreneurs producing goods either for export or domestic consumption had benefited from the boom of the last twenty years, as had the growing middle class, while for the most part, campesinos and workers had not.

The earliest opposition group to coalesce against the Porfiriato was the anarchosyndicalist Partido Liberal Mexicano (PLM, or Mexican Liberal Party) under the leadership of the brothers Enrique and Ricardo Flores Magón. Familiar with the miserable working conditions and capitalist exploitation in the United States and Mexico, the Flores Magóns were transnational protesters against Liberal modernization. Particularly active in the mining companies, the PLM published *Regeneración*, a newspaper that assailed the excesses of Porfirian capitalism, and particularly the poor treatment of Mexican workers. As the PLM pointed out, foreign employees enjoyed far higher pay and benefits, and they were paid in U.S. dollars. The answer to the problems of Mexican workers, the Flores Magón brothers believed, lay in radical social transformation.

The Flores Magóns knew that poverty, by itself, does not necessarily inspire revolutionary ideas. Instead, they were aware that the contrast between rich and poor that many Mexicans encountered in their everyday existence gradually impelled an increasing number of the poor toward violent opposition.

Therefore, the PLM found an unlikely fertile ground for followers among the workers of the Cananea copper mine in northeastern Sonora, only nine miles south of the Arizona border. Copper mining had arrived in Sonora on a grand scale during the 1890s, and in short order, it transformed the economy, demographics, and social relations in the state. Once a sleepy backwater at the frontier, Sonora emerged as a crucial nexus with the dynamic U.S. economy. The discovery of large copper deposits there brought significant U.S. investments to northern Sonora. In 1899, William E. Greene purchased the rights to a copper mine near Cananea, then a hamlet of two hundred inhabitants. Within six years, Cananea was home to the nation's largest copper mine as well as 15,000 inhabitants, and was now the third largest town in Sonora. Most of the inhabitants worked in the copper mine, and many of them had migrated to Cananea from all over Mexico. The reason for this huge influx of laborers was not only the abundance of available work, but also the miners' wages, which were twice as high as those in the rest of Mexico. Yet in 1906, it was these relatively well-paid miners who organized the first large-scale strike of the Porfirian era. Working side by side with foreign workers, and particularly U.S. engineers and managers, the Mexican miners experienced the effects of discrimination first hand, as their foreign counterparts enjoyed wages many times higher than their own. It was in this context of heightened material expectations and the glaring contrast between foreign white-collar employees and Mexican workers that the PLM found its adherents. In the spring of 1906, mine workers presented management with a series of demands, including higher wages and equal treatment of foreign and Mexican employees. The workers were responding to global events, and particularly the recent decline of silver prices, which had devalued the peso 50 percent against the gold-denominated U.S. dollar. Rudely rebuffed by management, labor organizers called a strike on June 1. When violence broke out, a detachment of rurales crushed the strike in brutal fashion, hanging strike leaders from trees and threatening the rest of the workers with conscription into the federal army unless they returned to work. Also involved in repressing the strike was a group of Arizona Rangers, who had crossed the border at the request of the Sonoran state government, a request that constituted a violation of Mexican national law.

Another source of opposition to the Porfiriato came from Mexico's campesinos. One case in point was Emiliano Zapata, an indigenous leader from the southern state of Morelos, who led an effort by his village and surrounding areas to reclaim the communal lands unfairly lost to agribusinesses, particularly sugar-producing estates. Since the 1880s, the sugar estates had claimed hundreds of thousands of acres under the Baldíos Law, and the process of land seizure had accelerated at the turn of the century. In the northern state of Chihuahua, campesinos had different grievances, seeking autonomy from a central government that had established its iron-fisted rule by means of the railroad. In an area in which Mexico City had once wielded only theoretical control, the railroad brought the intrusive presence of outsiders who were alien to the local culture and determined to subjugate the sparsely populated and arid region. We have already heard the voices of the Santa de Caborca and the villagers of Tomochic, but other Chihuahuan rebels such as Pascual Orozco and Pancho Villa would become even more famous in future years.

During the first decade of the 1900s, intellectuals and artists began to oppose the Díaz regime as well. Remarkably, even some of the intellectuals abandoned their close association with Díaz. As we have seen, Justo Sierra warned of the danger of keeping the indigenous population uneducated, and in 1909 Andrés Molina Enríquez identified the existence of large rural estates dedicated to agricultural export production as Mexico's greatest economic and social problem. Artists were even more biting in their critique: to this day, José Guadalupe Posada's *calaveras* (skulls) are popular representations of the corrupt upper class of Porfirian Mexico. Posada portrayed the elite as decadent corpses who preyed upon the poor majority and mimicked foreign culture.

The middle classes also played an important role in the making of an anti-Díaz coalition. Until 1905, artisans, doctors, lawyers, teachers, and other professionals had numbered among the principal beneficiaries of Liberal modernization. Beginning in 1906, however, the economic crisis occasioned by the decline in silver prices depreciated middle-class wages and salaries. In addition, the literate middle class resented the cronyism of the Díaz regime and aspired to wielding the political power that its economic significance appeared to demand. More than any other group, the middle class also demanded an end to the favoritism of foreign workers and investors.

Finally, at the top of the social ladder, regional elites—particularly those of the north—resented the Porfirian interference in state politics. These wealthy entrepreneurs impatiently awaited the demise of Díaz and the other gerontocrats in his inner circle. The landowner Francisco I. Madero, whose family had gotten rich by investing in the cotton boom in the northeastern state of Coahuila, was most significant among these elite figures. Emboldened by his family's material success, Madero had made a bid for the governorship of his native state, only to find out that a Díaz crony who enjoyed the unlimited support of the president stood in his way. As Madero found out, the Porfirian political structure had calcified, no longer allowing successful upstarts to find a niche in the hierarchy. In his growing opposition to Díaz, Madero rediscovered the Liberal traditions the positivists had discarded, including a commitment to individual liberties, democracy, and a greater measure of regional and local autonomy.

In 1908, Madero and other Díaz opponents thought that they would finally get an opportunity to challenge the aging dictator. Don Porfirio had granted an exclusive interview to the U.S. journalist James Creelman, who published his highly favorable account of the meeting in *Pearson's Magazine* in March 1908. This article quoted Díaz as announcing that Mexico was ready for democracy, and that he would not run for an eighth term as president in the 1910 elections. According to Creelman, Díaz also encouraged the formation of an opposition party to his own so that genuinely contested elections might result at both the national and the regional levels. Not intended for Mexican consumption, the Creelman interview sent shock waves through the somnolent political elite. Supporters praised Díaz for his statesmanship, yet they worried about losing their perks unless they acted quickly to assure themselves a position in the post-Díaz landscape. Opponents breathed a sigh of relief at the article and prepared their campaigns for congressional deputy, senator, governor, or even president. Then, on May 30, 1908, Díaz announced that his friends had "convinced" him to run for president yet again. A few months later, he demonstrated that he was still the same dictator Mexicans had known for three decades, when he arrested the PLM leaders. Disappointed, Madero and others set their sights on the position of vice president, occupied by the unpopular and corrupt Sonoran Ramón Corral. (In 1901, a constitutional amendment had created the vice presidency as an office elected separately from that of the presidency.) But Díaz soon made clear that he would not allow the opposition such an opening, either, backing Corral for a second term.

In 1909, Madero penned a scathing indictment of the Porfiriato, particularly its aging and repressive political leadership, in a book whose title translates as *The Presidential Succession of 1910*. It demanded that Díaz step aside in favor of a freely elected successor, who in turn would restore the principle of "no reelection" to the constitution. Madero soon thereafter decided that he would be the opposition candidate to challenge the Díaz regime. *The Presidential Succession* was the first mass-produced political platform in Mexican history. In January 1910, Madero founded an opposition political party, the "Partido Antirreleccionista" (Anti-Reelectionist Party) and toured much of the country canvassing support for his candidacy. Everywhere, he spoke to widespread applause, and his support came from the middle classes as well as workers and campesinos. Díaz was so concerned about Madero's popularity that he had his opponent jailed on trumped-up charges shortly before the July 1910 elections.

Madero's campaign illustrated the extent and limits of Liberal modernization. In 1910, it was possible for a presidential candidate to tour the country by train, to speak to large crowds, among whom many knew how to read and write, and to use the telegraph for speedy communications. For the first time ever, many Mexicans—particularly the growing middle class—identified with their nation, as schools and public monuments advertised its official identity. Even women, long excluded from formal education outside convent walls, had made strides: in Sonora, one out of three students in the public schools was female. Yet modernity had not reached everyone, and it had come at a steep price. When Madero lambasted Díaz and his cronies for selling out their country to foreign investors, he spoke to a sympathetic audience that recognized the disparate treatment of Mexicans and foreigners. "Mexico: mother of foreigners and stepmother of Mexicans" had become a popular phrase largely because a much greater part of the population now identified itself as Mexican rather than in terms of local and/or regional allegiances. Madero's speeches also highlighted the discrepancy between the liberal democratic principles outlined in the Constitution of 1857 and the authoritarian practices of the Díaz regime. Finally, the majority—especially the rural poor, who made up almost two-thirds of the population—remained excluded from the benefits of modernization. As Madero pledged himself to redress centuries of injustice against Mexico's indigenous and poor mestizo population, he made only vague promises that showed he too belonged to the elite who had materially benefited from the Porfiriato. One could imagine a Mexico without don Porfirio, but how could a new regime address all of the grievances that had emerged over the previous decades?

CHAPTER FOUR

❧ The Mexican Revolution ❧

*I*n September 1910, the Díaz regime put on a grand show to commemorate the birthdays of the nation and the man who had ruled over it for so long. September 16 marked the centennial of the Hidalgo revolt that had begun the Wars of Independence, and don Porfirio celebrated his eightieth birthday five days later. The government spared no expense during the month-long festivities. It unveiled two massive monuments, the Angel of Independence and a monument to the niños héroes (boy heroes), at the Paseo de la Reforma and the entrance to Chapultepec Park, respectively. Foreign dignitaries and the Mexican upper class were treated to lavish balls overflowing with cocktails and French champagne. Of course, not all Mexicans could partake in the celebrations, and authorities forcibly removed beggars from the streets to give the fancy districts of the capital the appearance of a European city. This show of self-congratulation epitomized what the Porfiriato had become. The wealthy delighted in the celebration and interpreted it as proof that Mexico had arrived as a modern nation. For the poor majority, however, the opulent fiestas were offensive. While the lucky few sampled caviar and champagne, most Mexicans could only afford tortillas and beans; as the wealthy stuffed themselves at interminable banquets, parties, and receptions, thousands of children were dying of malnutrition. The celebrations consumed more money than the year's national educational budget in a nation plagued by an adult illiteracy rate of 85 percent.

The extravaganza would be the last great fiesta the Díaz regime would see. On November 18, 1910, less than two months after the celebrations, shooting broke out in the city of Puebla. When the dust had cleared, the police had killed Aquiles Serdán, the local leader of the Anti-Reelectionists, and his family.

This bloodshed was only the opening skirmish in what was to become the first social revolution of the twentieth century. As it was, the death of Serdán came two days early, as Madero's Plan of San Luis Potosí had called for a rebellion against Díaz to begin at 6 PM on November 20. Authored in San Antonio, Texas, but backdated to avoid violating U.S. neutrality laws, the plan declared the 1910 elections null and void, proclaiming Madero provisional president. This plan initiated one of the great social revolutions of the twentieth-century world, a revolution that began with high hopes for creating a more democratic and fair society but soon disintegrated into chaos. It was not until the 1940s that a new system would replace the old one.

THE FIESTA OF BULLETS, 1910–1920

Madero's call to arms found its greatest response in the northern state of Chihuahua. Independently, dozens of Madero supporters mobilized and armed makeshift rebel armies. Although campesinos constituted the bulk of these armies, the rebel cause attracted Mexicans from all walks of life, such as day laborers, shopkeepers, beggars, and intellectuals. Their reasons for joining the fight reflected many of the popular grievances against the Porfiriato: the closed and authoritarian political system, the favoritism toward foreigners, the loss of local autonomy, and the poor treatment of workers. After a few weeks, three leaders emerged to direct the Chihuahuan movement: the lawyer Abraham González, the cattle rustler Pancho Villa, and the former muleteer Pascual Orozco, upon whom devolved the military leadership of the movement. Over the next two months, much of the countryside in Chihuahua fell under rebel control. By February, Orozco's victories convinced Madero that it was time to return to Mexico to take command of the rebellion. By then, his supporters had risen up in several other states. Still determined, the Díaz regime defended its control over the cities of Chihuahua, and elsewhere in Mexico the army held the rebels in check.

The turning point came in May 1911, when Orozco's forces seized the border town of Ciudad Juárez, Chihuahua, located across the Rio Grande from El Paso, Texas. He did so against the advice of Madero, who feared U.S. intervention in case the fighting spilled over into U.S. territory. Angry at Orozco's insubordination, Madero left Orozco out of his provisional cabinet that was named in Ciudad Juárez only a few days after the rebel victory. As a result, Madero's coalition was strained from the start. Nonetheless, the capture of Ciudad Juárez augured the quick demise of the Díaz regime. Disheartened by the defeat, the federal army fell apart, with thousands of troops deserting.

Díaz decided to negotiate with Madero and agreed to leave his post by the end of the month as proclaimed in the Treaty of Ciudad Juárez. On May 25, Díaz and Vice President Corral tendered their resignations. In accordance with the treaty, Foreign Secretary Francisco León de la Barra became interim president and convoked national elections for October 1911. Díaz boarded a ship for exile in Paris, and he reportedly warned that Madero had "unleashed a tiger; let's see if he can control it."

Indeed, the rebel victory had been almost too easy. While Madero supporters danced in the streets and celebrated the end of the dictatorship, the terms of the treaty left the federal army intact. Most Porfirian officials in the national government and bureaucracy remained in their offices. During his six-month term as interim president, de la Barra and his government assiduously prepared a transition that would ensure the survival of the Porfirian political and military machine. Moreover, regional rebel leaders soon confronted de la Barra with their demands. Orozco was still fuming over Madero's decision not to include him in his provisional cabinet, and he opposed de la Barra's interim government, which included a majority of Porfirian officials. In the southern Mexican state of Morelos, campesinos under the leadership of Emiliano Zapata demanded the return of all lands seized by agribusinesses since the 1860s. Zapata was especially incensed that both de la Barra and Madero demanded the disarmament of his supporters, and he refused to comply with these orders. He also met with Madero to gain his support for his ideas on land reform, only to be disappointed when the presidential candidate did not make such a commitment. Madero underestimated the serious nature of these disagreements within the victorious coalition and believed that he would come to terms with both Orozco and Zapata as soon as he was president. Optimistically, he thought that free and fair elections and respect for local autonomy gave all Mexicans a voice in the political process and hence guaranteed the future solution of the country's social as well as political problems.

Although Madero easily triumphed in the election, his delight at reaching the pinnacle of power was short-lived. Within his own ranks, he faced opposition from Francisco Vázquez Gómez, his vice presidential candidate of 1910 whom Madero had passed over as his running mate in favor of José María Pino Suárez. In Morelos, fighting had already begun following de la Barra's attempt to disarm the Zapata rebels by force. Weeks before the election, Madero supporters had attempted to rough up a Porfirian opposition candidate, General Bernardo Reyes, who went into exile bitter about what he saw as a betrayal of Madero's democratic principles. When Madero took office on November 6,

1911—almost a year after the beginning of the revolution—he already found powerful enemies arrayed against him.

The new government thus faced a series of revolts just weeks after its inauguration. First came Zapata's "Plan of Ayala" of November 25, which sought the overthrow of Madero and the restitution of campesino land. In mid-December, Reyes crossed into northeastern Mexico from his self-imposed exile in San Antonio. As Reyes could not muster the support he had anticipated, he surrendered to federal troops on Christmas Day. Almost simultaneously, Madero received word of the rebellion of Emilio Vázquez Gómez, brother of the man he had passed over for vice president. In each instance, Madero needed to rely on the Federales (federal army), which remained under the leadership of Porfirian officers such as General Victoriano Huerta, who had spent the fall attempting to disarm the Zapatistas.

Madero compounded these difficulties by implementing policies that disappointed his supporters. To address land and labor reform, he created a National Agrarian Commission and a Labor Department but funded neither agency sufficiently to accomplish real progress. He also failed to deliver on his promise to boost educational expenditures, which remained stuck below 8 percent of the national budget. Finally, Madero revealed an unfortunate nepotistic tendency, awarding lucrative government posts to members of his immediate family. The main accomplishment of his presidency was the opening of the political process, which allowed those on the outside of the Porfirian circle to compete freely for power. As a result, Mexicans did not hesitate to express their grievances, and whereas a more authoritarian and powerful president would have been able to put a lid on the opposition, Madero fell short of the expectations he had created.

In March 1912, Orozco took advantage of the growing discontent when he, too, rebelled against the government. Encouraged by Zapata's plan that recognized him as the leader of his movement, Orozco proclaimed one of his own (March 25) that attacked the Madero family for occupying numerous posts in the federal and state governments and demanded a ten-hour work day and higher wages. Orozco's plan also called for agrarian reform and the expropriation of the foreign-owned railroad system. Nonetheless, Orozco curried the favor of landowners in Chihuahua, and his ranks included many Porfirians who saw the rebellion as an opportunity to turn the tables on Madero. In April, Orozco assembled an army of eight thousand troops and marched them toward Mexico City. Near the Chihuahua-Durango border, Orozco routed the Federales under the command of José González Salas, Madero's Secretary of

War. Humiliated, González committed suicide. At that moment, the Porfirian military proved to be the president's best ally. Just when the fortunes of the Federales looked bleak, General Victoriano Huerta, a veteran Porfirian military officer, assumed control over the troops. In late May, the Federales defeated Orozco's forces at Casas Grandes, Chihuahua.

Huerta's triumph at Casas Grandes marked the emergence of two rising stars in the Mexican Revolution without whom he could not have won this significant military victory: Doroteo Arango Arámbula, better known as Pancho Villa, and Alvaro Obregón Salido. Both Villa and Obregón commanded volunteer forces that grew from detachments of a few hundred into the largest rebel armies that had ever existed in Mexico. Many details of the life of Villa, a legendary revolutionary hero, remain in dispute. He was born in the northern state of Durango in 1878 into an illiterate campesino family. He worked as a sharecropper at a very young age to support his family following his father's death, and first gained renown by murdering an hacienda owner who had attempted sexual assault on Arango's younger sister. Arango fled to the neighboring state of Chihuahua with the police in pursuit. By 1910, he as known as Pancho Villa, and he and his bandits operated in both his native state and in Chihuahua. Villa joined the revolution upon meeting Abraham González, Madero's representative in Chihuahua and future governor, and he fought to break the economic and political power of the large landowners. His counterpart, Obregón, was born in Huatabampo, Sonora, in 1880. Like Villa, Obregón grew up in poverty, although his mother was descended from a wealthy family. Unlike Villa, however, he managed to build up a modest agricultural enterprise producing chickpeas and other foods, and he occupied several minor posts at the end of the Porfirian era. He joined the campaign against Orozco upon the request of Sonoran governor José María Maytorena, who was concerned that the unrest in neighboring Chihuahua would mobilize poor campesinos in the eastern part of his native state. As a latecomer to the revolution, he therefore represented the ascendant middle class in northern Mexico—a group interested in political stability and economic development, but not necessarily in the redemption of landless campesinos.

It was Huerta, however, who took immediate advantage from the victory over Orozco at Casas Grandes. He had emerged as the guarantor of political stability, and Madero increasingly depended upon his services. Three months later, Madero confronted yet another rebellion, that of don Porfirio's nephew, Félix Díaz, who rose up in Veracruz with a call to the Federales to depose Madero. Captured and court-martialed, the younger Díaz received the death sentence, only to have it commuted to life in prison by the lenient President

Madero. Again, Huerta was instrumental in Díaz's defeat. Díaz was escorted to federal prison in Mexico City, where he established contact with another imprisoned rebel, General Reyes.

This fourth victory over rebel movements, not counting Zapata's ongoing insurrection, was to be Madero's last triumph. Díaz and Reyes spent several months plotting a coup from their separate prison cells, and on February 9, 1913, they escaped with the help of federal troops that had deserted to join their rebellion. Reyes died during the escape, but Díaz survived and directed his troops to march toward the National Palace, where Federales repelled them. The rebels then occupied the Ciudadela, or armory, west of downtown Mexico City. Once again, Madero turned to Huerta to quash this latest rebellion. By this point, however, Huerta had reached the conclusion that Madero was unfit to be president. Huerta negotiated with Díaz and allowed supplies to reach the Ciudadela, even as the Federales engaged the rebels. On February 18, he joined forces with Díaz in an agreement brokered by U.S. Ambassador Henry Lane Wilson and other foreign diplomats. Huerta had Madero and Pino Suárez arrested and forced their resignations, and a few hours later, Congress confirmed him as president. All at once, the gunfire in Mexico City ceased, and what has become known as the *decena trágica*—the Tragic Ten Days—had resulted in the defeat of Madero's democratic government. General Huerta was not content with usurping the presidency, however. Three days later, Madero and Pino Suárez were shot dead while Huerta's men were transporting them to prison. Although the exact details of the murders have never been elucidated, most evidence points to Huerta and/or Díaz as being responsible for the crime. A few days later, Huerta's minions assassinated Chihuahua governor Abraham González as well.

The deaths of Madero, Pino Suárez, and González only augured the spilling of more blood. The wealthy landowner Venustiano Carranza, the governor of Coahuila and a friend of the slain ex-president's family, denounced the coup in the Plan de Guadalupe, which proclaimed Carranza interim president. A few weeks later, the provisional state government of Sonora followed suit, declaring that it would not recognize the Huerta regime in Mexico City. To defend this decision, Obregón's volunteer army took the field to drive the Federales out of their garrisons throughout the state. In González's stead, Villa led the anti-Huerta forces in Chihuahua. In April 1913, representatives from all three of these northern movements met at Monclova, Coahuila, to sign a plan that named Carranza *primer jefe*, or First Chief, of what the rebels called the Constitutionalist Army. In the south, Zapata, whose forces had firsthand experience with Huerta's iron-fisted Federales, roundly rejected the new government and even ordered the execution of the agents sent to negotiate with him. As in the case of Madero's alliance, the loose coalition against Huerta represented widely divergent goals, and the rebels agreed on little other than his removal. Although most of them operated under the Constitutionalist umbrella, these rebels became known by the name of their leader. Thus the Carrancistas wished to restore Madero's short-lived democracy, the Villistas sought local autonomy and freedom from powerful landowners, the Zapatistas desired land reform, and the Obregonistas fought, among other things, for the freedom of their state from the interference of the central government. Initially, most of Mexico remained under Huerta's control, and the dictator even undertook some modest reform measures to co-opt the opposition. The governments of three great powers—Britain, France and Germany—were firmly in his corner.

Over the next year, however, the rebel forces began to gain ground against the Huerta regime. In Washington, the newly elected President Woodrow Wilson, a Democrat, disavowed the actions of the U.S. ambassador, who had been nominated by his Republican predecessor, William H. Taft. A former college professor, the intellectual Wilson supported a people's right to self-determination and democratic rule and opposed dictatorships such as Huerta's that had come to power through violence. Although Wilson initially embargoed the export of weapons to both Huerta and the Constitutionalists, the rebels controlled several strategic border towns and managed to smuggle arms across the border. In Chihuahua and Morelos, Villa's and Zapata's forces carried out effective guerrilla warfare and ransacked haciendas held by Huerta support-ers. In Chihuahua and Sonora, Villa's and Obregón's troops attacked Federal garrisons and gradually expanded the territory held by the Constitutionalist armies. This war proved far more brutal than the campaign against Díaz, and the longer the insurrection continued, the more the tide turned against Huerta. As casualties mounted, underpaid Federales deserted to the rebel armies, forces composed primarily of makeshift battalions of young volunteer fighters. For the first time in Mexican history, women played an active role in the fighting, and popular music and art commemorated the heroism of these female sol-diers, the *soldaderas*. In Mexico City, workers took up arms against the Huerta regime under the Casa del Obrero Mundial (House of the World's Worker), a radical labor union affiliated with the Industrial Workers of the World. In February 1914, Wilson allowed the Constitutionalists to purchase weapons in the United States. With the supply lines from the United States open, Obregón's and Villa's northern armies began to march on central Mexico. In particular, Villa's División del Norte, or Division of the North, became the largest rebel army, larger than those of Carranza, Obregón, and Zapata combined. Once again—as in the nineteenth century—central authority had disintegrated in favor of regional warlords.

The U.S. government played a significant role in hastening Huerta's demise. In April 1914, Mexican officials in Tampico, a Gulf Coast city still held by the Federales, arrested a group of nine visiting U.S. soldiers stationed on a gunboat offshore, reportedly for entering a prohibited zone. Incensed, U.S. commander Henry Mayo demanded a twenty-one gun salute to the United States flag on Mexican soil and the punishment of those responsible for the arrests. Huerta apologized but refused to salute the U.S. flag. As tempers flared, Wilson on April 20 requested congressional authorization to use force to obtain the apology Mayo had demanded. The following day, Wilson awoke to learn that the German gunboat *Ypiranga* was approaching the harbor of Veracruz, Mexico's major Gulf Coast port, to unload a shipment of weapons for Huerta at Veracruz later that day. In an effort to keep the Germans, future enemies in World War I, from supplying the Federales, Wilson immediately ordered the U.S. occupation of Veracruz, Mexico's principal port. He did so without consulting either Huerta or Carranza, the nominal head of the insurrection. Although Carranza complained loudly, his faction gained the most from the incident, as Carrancista forces operated close to the city and moved in shortly after the U.S. occupation. Carranza set up his provisional government in Veracruz long before the Marines departed in November 1914. The U.S. occupation of Veracruz was therefore very significant for the revolution. It gave a decisive boost to the Carranza faction; it led to an outburst of nationalist fervor that would later find its expression in the Constitution of 1917; it broke Huerta's sole supply line from his allies in Europe; and it demoralized the Federales. In June, Villa seized the strategically significant silver mining town of Zacatecas, and one month later, Huerta went into exile as Carranza's and Obregón's forces occupied Mexico City.

Unfortunately, once again, internal divisions rendered asunder the revolutionary coalition that had united to overthrow a dictator. At the beginning of the war against Huerta, Carranza had claimed the title of provisional president under the Plan of Guadalupe, and the Monclova Convention, which both Obregón and Villa had signed, had designated him primer jefe. But Zapata was not a party to this agreement, and Villa resented Wilson's favoritism toward Carranza as evidenced by the U.S. occupation of Veracruz. Villa also regarded Carranza as an aristocratic, conservative landowner, and he believed that Carranza had once given him military directives to stop his southward advance in order to allow his own and Obregón's armies to reach Mexico City before the División del Norte did. For his part, Carranza considered Villa merely a bandit, and he arrogantly refused to negotiate with him on equal terms. At the same time, in early August 1914, the beginning of World War I complicated matters, as the Germans sought to play the Mexican revolutionary factions against one another.

This was actually the case, anyway, even without much German assistance. Tempers flew at the Convention of Aguascalientes of October 1914, convened to discuss the political future. Each of the four major factions sent a number of delegates to this convention that corresponded to their military strength. Villa's was by far the largest army, thus his delegates moved to terminate Carranza as primer jefe and to select one of their men, Eulalio Gutiérrez, as provisional president. Incensed about the convention's decision to pass over Carranza for the presidency, the Carrancistas walked out of the meeting. Obregón initially waffled and then entered into negotiations with Villa. These talks ended with Villa making death threats to Obregón, and the Sonoran ultimately sided with Carranza, while Zapata allied with Villa. Because they recognized Gutiérrez as the president chosen by the Convention of Aguascalientes, the Zapatistas and Villistas became known as Conventionists, while their adversaries kept the name Constitutionalists.

The following year was the bloodiest in modern Mexican history. The war between the factions pitted Villa's and Zapata's campesinos against a city-based alliance with national goals. While the Conventionists never defined common goals, Carranza operated a provisional national government in Veracruz that passed laws ending debt peonage and promising labor reform to workers. In February 1915, Obregón made a crucial agreement with the Casa del Obrero Mundial that gained him the support of the union's Red Battalions, the armed workers who had played an important role in defeating the Huerta regime. The Casa saw Obregón as a logical ally. The general had demonstrated a radical streak during his army's occupation of Mexico City after Huerta's fall, when he had imposed special taxes on the rich and forced those unwilling to pay them to sweep the streets. The outcome of the fighting was decided in April and May 1915 at the battles of Celaya and León, where Obregón's machine guns mowed down the Villistas on horseback. Eager to back the winner, the Wilson administration gravitated toward the Constitutionalists, allowing arms shipments to Carranza's and Obregón's forces and awarding Mexico de facto diplomatic recognition in October 1915.

But Villa, reduced to a few hundred supporters, was not quite finished fighting and decided to draw Mexico into an international conflict. He was incensed that the U.S. government had recognized and supported the Consti-

tutionalists. For example, in the fall of 1915, the Wilson administration had allowed Obregón's troops to make a loop across southern Arizona in order to elude Conventionist forces in neighboring Sonora and then attack them from the rear. To exact revenge and to incite a conflict between the United States and Mexico that would weaken his enemies, on March 9, 1916, Villa's men sacked Columbus, New Mexico, in the only attack on the continental United States in the twentieth century. Wilson responded by sending a "Punitive Expedition" into Chihuahua, the second time in two years that his administration had decided to undertake a military intervention in Mexico. The invasion force under the leadership of General William Pershing chased Villa across Chihuahua but failed to capture him. The Punitive Expedition made Villa into a popular hero, someone who had stood up to the United States and gotten away with it. Although Villa never regained his prior significance in Mexican politics, he had acquired new value as a patriot.

The Punitive Expedition also angered Carranza, who responded by making nationalist speeches that assailed the privileges of foreigners in Mexico. So strained were relations between Wilson and Carranza that German diplomats sought to exploit these tensions for their own benefit in World War I. As British intelligence learned by way of an intercepted telegraph communication, the Zimmermann Telegram, the German government authorized its diplomatic representatives to approach Carranza with an offer of a German-Mexican alliance in case of war between the United States and Mexico. Written at a time when the United States still remained neutral in the war, the Zimmermann Telegram even included assurances that Germany would support Mexico in the recovery of all lands lost to the United States during the nineteenth century. Carranza did not respond to these German overtures, but Wilson's ensuing declaration of war—a declaration facilitated in large part by the public outcry in the United States over the intercepted telegram—indirectly came to his assistance. Following the U.S. entry into World War I in April 1917, Wilson withdrew Pershing's battle-tested troops from Chihuahua to deploy them in France against the German army.

Meanwhile, the Constitutionalists turned to the difficult project of national reconstruction. When the fighting was ended, much of the country lay in ruins. Paper currency was now worthless, overland trade had broken down in many areas, and the revolutionaries had blown up railroad tracks and port facilities. Carranza and Obregón also knew that the revolution had transcended its earlier, narrowly political goals. Obregón's alliance with the Casa del Obrero Mundial promised assistance to labor unions, and in January 1915 Carranza had proclaimed his support for comprehensive land reform.

State governors close to Obregón such as Salvador Alvarado of Yucatán and Plutarco Elías Calles of Sonora issued decrees favorable to workers, and they increased taxation on foreign-owned companies. But Carranza and Obregón disagreed on how to address these social and nationalist demands, and their discord manifested itself during the Constitutional Convention held in the city of Querétaro in central Mexico between late 1916 and early 1917. The convention was composed of Constitutionalist delegates from all states, primarily civilians with university degrees. Carranza charged the convention with updating the liberal Constitution of 1857 and asked the delegates to elect him president in the absence of general national elections. But Obregón's representatives viewed the redrafting of the constitution as a vehicle for economic and social change. They inserted clauses into the new document that sought to provide guarantees for Mexican workers and campesinos while abrogating the special privileges of the Catholic Church and foreign investors. Article 3 of the constitution reiterated the commitment to a secular society, one in which the Church would tend only to the souls of its parishioners rather than play a political role in the country. In an attempt to repeal the reforms of the 1880s that had facilitated the foreign acquisition of vast land holdings and mining enterprises, Article 27 proclaimed the land and the subsoil the patrimony of the Mexican nation, for use by foreigners only upon application to and the consent of the federal government. Article 27 also promised a land reform to benefit landless campesinos. Article 33 threatened foreigners who refused to submit to Mexican law with extradition, and Article 123 provided important guarantees to workers, including an eight-hour day and a six-day week. Approved on February 5, 1917, the new constitution was the first in the entire world that contained a social agenda.

If the drafting of the new constitution had gone relatively smoothly, implementing its new provisions was a different matter. Putting these into practice would have not only antagonized foreign investors, but also Mexican proprietors and the Catholic Church. For the moment, Carranza decided not to enforce the radical changes of the constitution. Free to act in Mexico after its victory alongside the western Allies in World War I in November 1918, the U.S. government weighed in against implementation of Article 27, putting Carranza further on the defensive.

Frustrated on that front, Carranza focused on reasserting central control over the regional warlords who, true to form, had taken advantage of the revolution to carve out independent spheres of power. Apart from Villa in Chihuahua, Carranza confronted Félix Díaz in Oaxaca and Zapata in Morelos. The latter proved to be the biggest thorn in Carranza's side, having already

defied Díaz, Madero, and Huerta, so Carranza decided to get rid of him. On April 10, 1919, a Carranza ally lured Zapata to the hacienda of Chinameca, in the state of Morelos, under the pretext of intending to desert to the Zapatistas. When Zapata entered the hacienda, Carranza's loyalists gunned him down. The president then moved against Obregón, who had returned to Sonora, where his allies Plutarco Elías Calles and Adolfo de la Huerta led a state government too radical for Carranza's taste. Behind the scenes, Carranza attempted to choose his own successor, who was slated to be elected by popular vote in 1920. Now he prepared to spurn the presidential ambitions of Obregón, who had helped him win the war between the factions, in favor of the bland Ignacio Bonillas, a civilian and the Mexican ambassador to the United States. In April 1920, Carranza sent a military expedition to Sonora, an action Governor de la Huerta interpreted as an attempt to unseat him.

Carranza's challenge to Obregón and the other Sonorans, however, led to his own downfall and the last violent change of power until the present day. De la Huerta and Calles responded to the provocation of the federal government with the Plan de Agua Prieta, which withdrew recognition from the Carranza government and called for its overthrow. Within a month, Obregón and General Pablo González, who harbored presidential aspirations of his own, had chased Carranza out of the capital. Carranza fled by train to Puebla, whence he hoped to reach Veracruz, which previously proved hospitable to his political ambitions. But the rebels had blown up the railroad track, and when the train stopped east of Puebla Carranza and his entourage were forced to continue the trip on horseback. On the evening of May 20, 1920, Carranza's group arrived in the small village of Tlaxcalantongo in the Sierra Madre. By the next morning, the party had been attacked, most likely by Obregón supporters, and Carranza lay dead. We will probably never know the circumstances of the president's death, but it proved a significant watershed. Not only was it the last assassination of a sitting president in Mexican history, but it ushered in more than two decades of consolidation that defined the extent of revolutionary change.

CONSOLIDATION UNDER THE SONORAN DYNASTY, 1920–1934

It fell to the three Sonoran leaders who headed the Agua Prieta rebellion—de la Huerta, Obregón, and Calles, a trio also known as the "Sonoran Triangle"—to lead the consolidation of the new regime during the 1920s and early 1930s. The effort involved placating a U.S. government determined to protect foreign property rights, confronting armed challenges from disaffected revolutionary leaders, meeting the heightened expectations of workers and campesinos, and promoting a national consciousness to displace regional loyalties.

The task of consolidation was a momentous one. Many regions were devastated after a decade of military conflict that had left between 500,000 and 2 million Mexicans dead. The revolution also had exacted a great toll on the country's infrastructure: agriculture lay in shambles, and many mines had stopped operating. Protected by caciques paid off by foreign investors, only the oil industry operated close to full capacity. The Sonoran Triangle also confronted significant popular mobilization and heightened expectations for their own agendas from those who had participated in the revolution. Depending on their background and motivation, each revolutionary group advocated a unique set of aims from among a wide array of choices such as land reform, democracy, education, better working conditions, national control over resources, and indigenous people's and women's rights. The latter issue, in particular, became increasingly important in the course of the 1920s and 1930s, as women pushed for the right to vote—a right that they would not be granted until 1953.

The Sonoran leaders could not please all of these revolutionaries, and in fact, they had no intention of doing so. As inhabitants of a border state the population and economy of which had grown rapidly during the Porfiriato, they intended to reform rather than overthrow Mexico's capitalist system. Their priority consisted of national reconstruction, and they desired to forge a new national consciousness among all Mexicans. The Sonorans emphasized public education as a way to instill patriotic pride in Mexican children and to counteract the pervasive influence of the Catholic Church, which they (like the nineteenth-century Liberals) regarded as a foreign-led, reactionary institution. They wished to implement those aspects of the new constitution that put Mexicans on an equal footing with foreigners, and they intended to improve working conditions so as to foster the growth of the urban middle class. They also decreed land reform in areas controlled by their political enemies (but not necessarily where it was most needed), and Calles planned a campaign for public health and morality that would stamp out prostitution, drinking, and games of chance. Yet on this last point, the Sonorans revealed the internal contradictions of their program from the very beginning. In July 1920, the Sonorans sent a military expedition under General Abelardo Rodríguez to the border territory of Baja California, then under the control of a cacique who profited from the brothels and casinos of Tijuana. Rodríguez immediately closed down these operations, only to launch his own casinos in close affiliation with U.S. investors. Demanding unswerving loyalty from their fellow Mexicans, the Sonorans (and particularly Obregón and Calles) were authoritarian, yet reform-oriented leaders of a nation they believed to be once again threatened with dissolution.

De la Huerta took his first turn at the presidency serving as interim president between May and November 1920. His brief tenure was marked by significant efforts to make peace with the enemies of the Sonorans. The interim president succeeded in getting Pancho Villa to agree to lay down his arms in exchange for the grant of an hacienda in the northern state of Durango. In July 1920, de la Huerta organized the first national elections since 1911, which Obregón won by a large margin. In the Obregón administration, de la Huerta became Finance Secretary, and Calles, Secretary of Gobernación, or the interior.

From the outset, Obregón confronted an intractable problem: the absence of U.S. diplomatic recognition, withheld since the Agua Prieta rebellion with the justification that the Sonorans had violated the Mexican constitution in overthrowing Carranza by the force of arms. Without diplomatic recognition, the Mexican government could not purchase arms and supplies in the United States, and rebels could freely organize over the border as the U.S. Neutrality Laws only applied to recognized governments. The U.S. government understood the importance of the recognition issue and used it in an attempt to extract concessions from the Sonoran Triangle. U.S.-owned businesses had suffered multimillion-dollar losses during the revolution, so foreign oil companies and landowners demanded the continuation of the generous concessions awarded to them during the Porfiriato. Further, President Wilson condemned the Agua Prieta rebellion as a coup d'état against an elected government. His successor, Republican President Warren G. Harding, was not about to award diplomatic recognition to the Mexican regime without substantial guarantees in regard to U.S. land claims and property rights in Mexico. In particular, Harding demanded the partial suspension of the provisions of Article 27 of the revolutionary constitution as they applied to U.S. investors, so they could continue to drill solely on land that they owned. With the subsoil once again the property of the nation under Article 27, the oil companies faced high production taxes and perhaps even expropriation. Even worse for the Sonorans, both Harding and the chair of the U.S. Senate's Foreign Relations Committee, Albert B. Fall of New Mexico, enjoyed close ties to the oil companies. As if the stakes were not high enough, Mexican oil production continued to rise, and in 1921 the country was the world's largest producer of crude oil. Throughout 1921 and 1922, de la Huerta vainly attempted to secure U.S. diplomatic recognition for Mexico in return for a commitment to pay a large portion of U.S. claims.

In the absence of U.S. diplomatic recognition, Obregón initially continued de la Huerta's cautious policies of pacification and reconciliation. He moved military commanders around different regions to break the local strongholds many of them had acquired during the decade of fighting. He also shed his reputation as an enemy of the propertied classes, pointing to his own onetime exploits as a chickpea farmer in an effort to portray himself as a moderate and a capitalist, and to encourage the flow of both foreign and domestic investment capital. At the same time, organized labor and agrarian organizations played an ever-increasing role in the Obregón administration. In particular, his presidency witnessed the rise of the Confederación Regional Obrera Mexicana (CROM, or Mexican Regional Workers' Confederation) under the leadership of the flamboyant Luis Napoleón Morones. Morones enjoyed a close relationship to Calles, whose star rose rapidly during the Obregón years.

Without a doubt, Calles was the most controversial among the great leaders of the revolution. The scion of a once-wealthy family, he grew up in Hermosillo, Sonora, as an adopted child. He spent his early adulthood trying his hand at a variety of occupations, serving as a teacher, hotel manager, farmer, and mill operator. At the outbreak of the Revolution, he found himself in his native city of Guaymas, where he supported the local movement in favor of Madero. Upon Madero's triumph, Calles was appointed police chief of the border town of Agua Prieta, a post he retained until General Huerta's coup. Thereafter, he joined the Constitutionalist army and allied himself with both Carranza and Obregón. In 1915, Carranza named him provisional governor of Sonora, and Calles distinguished himself both in his zeal for reforms and in his commitment to rid his home state of his political enemies. In 1919, he joined Carranza's cabinet as Secretary of Commerce, Industry, and Labor, and he served in important positions under both de la Huerta and Obregón, building alliances with labor boss Morones and other revolutionary leaders.

As Obregón's protégé, Calles enjoyed the inside track in the presidential election of 1924. Indeed, Obregón's decision to support Calles was the first example of the *dedazo*, or finger point, the practice of the outgoing president choosing his successor. With few exceptions, this practice would endure for the remainder of the twentieth century. Calles's presidential campaign was the first to employ mass media such as radio, and it featured widespread travel through the republic. Yet it also elicited the opposition of two different and powerful groups: military leaders close to Obregón who believed themselves more worthy of the presidency than Calles, and civilian members of Congress who resented the imposition of a president from above. Calles opponents found an opening when the relationship between Obregón and Finance Minister de la Huerta deteriorated following the July 1923 assassination of Pancho Villa. De la Huerta blamed this murder on Calles and Obregón, both of whom had opposed the amnesty he had conferred upon Villa when he was interim president. In November of that year, de la Huerta resigned from his post following Obregón's and Calles's interference in the gubernatorial elections in the central state of San Luis Potosí. Soon thereafter, Calles's enemies nominated the former Finance Minister as their candidate for the 1924 elections. As is often the case in Mexico, however, the question of who would hold the presidency was decided on the battlefield rather than by the ballot box. In December 1923, de la Huerta led a rebellion against Obregón and Calles that counted on almost 60 percent of all senior officers in the army. But Obregón and Calles had powerful allies, and they had recently secured U.S. diplomatic recognition in exchange for a pledge not to apply the Constitution of 1917 retroactively against U.S. investors as a result of the so-called Bucareli Accords. Thus government troops enjoyed the benefit of a steady flow of arms and ammunition from the United States, while the rebels were denied the same benefit. In March 1924, Obregón and his allies scored decisive victories over the Delahuertistas. Four months later, Calles was elected president with more than 82 percent of the vote.

Whereas Obregón had overcome the frayed relations with the United States in large part by his unequivocal hold over domestic politics, Calles entered office in the opposite situation. His government enjoyed U.S. diplomatic recognition, and even before he took office, Calles was fêted during an extended international tour that took him to the United States, France, and Germany. Yet Calles lacked authority at home. As a result of the elections, candidates loyal to Obregón had taken the majority of congressional seats, and the new president could only count on the unswerving loyalty of Morones's Partido Laborista Mexicano (PLM, or Mexican Labor Party) as well as that of a small agrarian party. Many Mexicans still viewed his presidency as an imposition, and Calles lacked the widespread popularity of his two Sonoran predecessors.

As a result, Calles decided to press ahead with a full slate of reforms in order to make his own mark. He was most concerned with putting government finances on a solid footing; his first year in office witnessed the creation of the Banco de México, the country's first official bank of issue; a comprehensive tax reform; and a drastic reduction in the public debt. Calles also embarked on measures designed to improve the national infrastructure such as rural electrification and road building. The latter task was particularly important in a decade that witnessed the coming of the automobile, the new status symbol of the middle class throughout Europe and the Americas.

To complement these measures aimed at national economic development and the enhancement of central control, the president pursued populist policies appealing to labor and nationalists alike. He signed legislation forcing the foreign-owned oil companies to apply for confirmatory concessions to renew their right to exploit the Mexican subsoil. This legislation abridged existing contracts, many of them signed during the Porfirian era, and it included a significant tax increase. Calles also supported a progressive government in the Central American nation of Nicaragua, a government that had come to power following the end of thirteen years of U.S. occupation. U.S. business interests were not pleased with Calles. By June 1925, Secretary of State Frank B. Kellogg had declared that Mexico was "on trial before the world" and demanded that the Calles administration meet all of its international obligations. The press of media tycoon William R. Hearst was even more strident, portraying Calles as a Bolshevik seeking to transform his country in the image of Soviet Russia. The president, however, adroitly defended his position by stating that the Mexican people had the right to make their own laws, whether or not the U.S. government approved of them.

The Calles presidency is best remembered for its campaign against the Catholic Church. Indeed, an unforgiving anticlericalism was the president's most abiding conviction, as Calles viewed his campaign against the Church as a continuation of the nineteenth-century Reforma. Under Porfirio Díaz, the Church had accommodated itself to Liberal rule and regained much of its previous significance. The Sonorans were committed to keep the Church out of public life, a commitment that included the prohibition of outdoor religious ceremonies in public spaces, a mainstay of popular religion, but forbidden under the new Constitution, which restricted the use of plazas and streets. For example, Mexicans worship outdoors during Holy Week processions, on November 2 (the Day of the Dead) and on December 12 (Guadalupe Day). During Calles's presidency, hostilities erupted in 1926 after the publication of an interview with the Mexican archbishop in the newspaper *El Universal*, in which the archbishop was quoted as an unforgiving opponent of the Revolution. The government struck at the Church with the Calles Law, which required all priests to register with local authorities and limited their number to one in 10,000 inhabitants. The Church could not accept these strictures on their activities. On July 31, 1926, the archbishop retaliated by suspending all masses and other religious ceremonies.

This action precipitated the largest social revolt of the 1920s and 1930s, the Cristero Rebellion. In August 1926, all over central and western Mexico, devout campesinos took up arms to the cry of "Viva Cristo Rey," or "Long Live Christ the King!" By the end of the year, nearly 30,000 rebel forces were in arms against the government. Commanded by an able Porfirian officer, the Cristeros seized large swathes of two central Mexican states, Jalisco and Michoacán. In vain, the Calles regime attempted to counterattack by painting itself as a force for social progress and friend of the campesinos against an exploitative, foreign-led institution. Independent family farms abounded in the heartland of the Cristeros, and many smallholders feared rather than welcomed the specter of land reform. In this devout region, home to the largest concentration of clergy in all of Mexico and today a stronghold of the governing party, the Catholic PAN, inhabitants identified an attack on the Church with an attack on their way of life.

The Cristero Rebellion dealt a fatal blow to Calles's reform aspirations. Simultaneously, U.S.-Mexican relations plunged to a new low. U.S. Ambassador James R. Sheffield parroted Hearst's allegation that the Mexican Revolution was "Bolshevik"; the United States and Mexico clashed over Nicaragua, where both governments backed different sides in a bitter civil war, and U.S. Catholics pressed President Calvin Coolidge to stop what they viewed as the persecution of the Church in Mexico. The situation became so serious that Coolidge replaced Sheffield with the more conciliatory Dwight Morrow, reportedly enjoining the new ambassador to "keep us out of war with Mexico." By that time, a serious economic crisis devastated the national budget, as the prices of silver and other export products once again plunged.

As a result, the last two years of the Calles presidency witnessed the reemergence of Obregón, still the master of the Mexican army. Obregón desired to return to the presidency after the end of Calles's term even though Article 81 of the revolutionary constitution expressly outlawed reelection. That was not a problem for the former president, however. He used his extensive connections to most of the preeminent political figures on the national level to amend Article 81 to permit reelection as long as terms were not consecutive. Obregón's next hurdle—the candidacy of two generals from the Sonoran coalition, Arnulfo Gómez and Francisco R. Serrano—posed a more serious obstacle. Mindful of Porfirio Díaz's example, many Mexicans disapproved of Obregón's bid to return to the presidency and threw their support behind the strongman's rivals. Whether either one of them would have topped Obregón in the July 1928 elections is anyone's guess, as the government apprehended and assassinated both of them.

After causing so much bloodshed, Obregón himself fell victim to the bullets of an assassin. On July 17, 1928, less than two weeks after his election to a second term, a fanatical Catholic, José de León Toral, approached Obregón at a luncheon given in his honor and fired five bullets into his chest. It was the final chapter in a bloody cycle that had claimed the lives of all major revolutionary leaders: Madero, Zapata, Carranza, Villa, and Obregón. Interrogated under torture, Toral proclaimed to have acted alone, driven by religious convictions. As police investigators found out, Toral was part of a religious circle convened by the religious mystic Concepción Acevedo y de Llata, better known as Madre Conchita, the Mother Superior of a convent in Mexico City. Many Obregón supporters, however, were not satisfied with this explanation and blamed the outgoing president or Labor Secretary Morones for the assassination. Although no historical document points to Calles's or Morones's complicity in the murder, the allegations finished the political career of Morones and impelled Calles to try to craft a political system in which he did not play a direct role.

In what was probably Calles's most adroit move of his long career, the president used the occasion of his last state of the nation address, or *informe*, to outline this new political system; one in which he was to play a significant role. Calles proclaimed that Mexico was in transition from the age of caudillos to the age of institutional rule, and he announced that he would not seek another term as president. Shortly thereafter, Calles and his allies crafted a ruling party, the Partido Nacional Revolucionario (PNR, or National Revolutionary Party). Founded in February 1929, the PNR would rule Mexico under three different names until the end of the century, the world's longest-ruling party with the exception of the Communist Party of the Soviet Union. Initially, the PNR was a confederation of regional revolutionary parties whose bosses pledged loyalty to the national government. Over time, the regional parties—products of the 1910s, when regional warlords held sway over much of Mexico—disappeared along with the independent power of these caciques.

Over the next six years, Calles continued to exert significant influence from behind the scenes as the so-called jefe máximo, or Supreme Chief, of the Mexican Revolution. During these years, a period that is known as the Maximato, three different presidents—Emilio Portes Gil, Pascual Ortiz Rubio, and Abelardo L. Rodríguez—occupied the presidential chair while Calles remained the ultimate arbiter of national political life. Under the guise of the PNR, the Jefe Máximo hired and fired governors, cabinet members, and even presidents; in particular, his personal intervention ended the reign of Ortiz Rubio in September 1932. Not for nothing did Mexicans call Ortiz Rubio and the other two Maximato presidents the *peleles*, or puppets.

During these years, Calles and his allies crafted a powerful myth of the revolution: the idea that the PNR represented the "revolutionary family," with the Jefe Máximo at its head. The notion of the revolutionary family implied a unified purpose of the revolution that had never existed, and it claimed that the PNR and its leaders represented this purpose. In its idealized version of the story, the main protagonists of the fiesta of bullets—Madero, Zapata, Villa, Carranza, and Obregón—had met a violent death, but the martyrdom of these heroes had not been in vain, as the ruling party still represented all of their aspirations: democracy, social justice, nationalism, and economic development. Two significant monuments in Mexico City advanced this idea. Less than two miles west of the city center, the unfinished Legislative Palace building commissioned by the Porfirians became the Monumento a la Revolución, an arch that housed the remains of all of these slain leaders except Obregón. Later on, the remains of Calles and Cárdenas joined those of Carranza, Madero, Zapata, and Villa. And on the very site of Obregón's death arose the Monumento al General Alvaro Obregón. The monument not only featured the original floor of the restaurant where Obregón had been shot, complete with bullet holes, but also a container with the general's arm, lost as a result of a Villista hand grenade during the decisive battles of 1915.

The myth of the revolutionary family was but one effort to promote national consciousness in Mexico. Another was the rise of revolutionary art, especially the mural paintings of Diego Rivera, Pascual Orozco, and David Alfaro Siqueiros. Rivera was the most influential of these artists. Beginning in the Obregón administration, he adorned the interior of government-owned buildings with colorful murals that depicted a revolutionary vision of Mexican history. But it was not until the Maximato that Rivera painted his most grandiose work inside the National Palace, a canvas of Mexico's history from the Aztecs to the twentieth century. Whether literate or not, visitors to the National Palace could see and understand the greatness of Tenochtitlán, the violence and blood of the conquest, and the oppression and social injustice of the Porfiriato. The mural was part of an effort to provide adult education to Mexicans, many of whom could not read and write, and to illustrate the reasons the revolutionaries had taken up arms against the Díaz regime as well as the government's vision of the future. Rivera's masterpiece even criticized the government for not bringing about the change it had promised.

The work of Rivera's wife, Frida Kahlo, constitutes another great example of revolutionary art—albeit one that was less appreciated until she became an international cultural icon after her death in 1955. The victim of a crippling streetcar accident at the age of seventeen, Kahlo was the daughter of a German photographer and a Mexican mother. Drawing on Mexican religious folk art, her paintings represented her own pain and suffering. The paintings—many of them self-portraits—display fractured and broken human bodies. Kahlo's work rejected traditional notions of gender in challenging the idea that women (following the lead of the Virgin Mary) must bear their suffering silently.

Fulfilling revolutionary promises became ever more difficult during the Great Depression, which followed "Black Friday" on October 29, 1929. This unprecedented stock market crash led to the implosion of the U.S. and European economies and caused mass bankruptcies and layoffs. It also drastically decreased demand for raw materials from Latin America. The Great Depression added to Mexico's existing economic woes caused by the decline of the silver price in 1926. It also led to the forced repatriation of more than 100,000 Mexicans and Chicanos, including thousands of U.S. citizens of Mexican descent. In 1930 alone, the Mexican economy contracted by 4 percent. The depression challenged elected leaders worldwide, contributing to Franklin D. Roosevelt's defeat of U.S. President Herbert Hoover in the 1932 presidential elections as well as the triumph of Adolf Hitler's Nazi party in Germany the following year. In Mexico, the crisis aggravated an already dire fiscal situation. Between 1930 and 1932, federal revenue dropped 25 percent in real terms. Real wages fell as well, producing hundreds of wildcat strikes in a country in which the Sonorans had long managed to quell labor discontent.

In Mexico, the Great Depression coincided with a low point of the revolution, as Calles and his allies confronted the crisis by means of heavy-handed repression, while flaunting their own increasing fortunes. The great heroes of the revolution were dead, and those who had survived appeared hopelessly corrupt, as they had used the years of revolution to amass great personal wealth. By the early 1930s, several leaders, including President Rodríguez, who held a significant stake in a posh casino in Tijuana, had become multimillionaires. Calles himself bought a swanky mansion and steadily moved toward the political right. In 1931, he announced that land reform had failed and that the party needed to embrace commercial agriculture rather than collective farming. He also increasingly clashed with workers' organizations, and particularly those independent of the CROM under Morones, such as the powerful railroad workers' union. Only in the area of the Church did Calles remain steadfast in his views. Although Morrow had helped Calles and President Portes Gil find a negotiated solution to the Cristero conflict in 1929, five years later, Calles incited his allies to another campaign against the Church. In 1934, he announced in Guadalajara: "The revolution is not over.... It is necessary to enter into a new period, one I would call the period of the psychological revolution. We have to enter and take possession of the conscience of children and youths, because they belong and should belong to the revolution.... [The revolution must] uproot the prejudices and form the new national soul."

But the Calles who attempted to rekindle the embers of the Church-state conflict in 1934 was but a shadow of his former self. His health had declined, and the Jefe Máximo spent more and more time in distant locales far away from Mexico City. As a result of this trend, President Rodríguez enjoyed far greater leeway than had his two predecessors, and the PNR leadership gradually began to distance itself from Calles. During the Rodríguez administration, the party recognized the degree to which it had abandoned the goals for which countless Mexicans had lost their lives. In 1933, the party adopted a progressive Six-Year Plan promising to bring greater benefits to campesinos and workers. At the same convention where the PNR delegates approved this plan, they also picked a presidential candidate for the period 1934–40: Calles's friend and protégé Lázaro Cárdenas del Río. Most Mexicans thought that this nomination represented business as usual, and few observers expected Cárdenas, who had always remained loyal to the Jefe Máximo, to break from the mold of his predecessors.

THE CÁRDENAS ERA AND BEYOND, 1934–1946

Cárdenas, however, was to prove far more independent than any one could have expected. Born in 1895 in the town of Jiquilpan, Michoacán, Cárdenas was part of a younger generation of revolutionaries, a generation dubbed the "cubs of the revolution." His cohort had come of age during the fiesta of bullets, but they had not served in leading roles during the 1910s. As mid-ranking officers, they had first-hand experiences with the rank and file of the revolution, and they knew why ordinary Mexicans had risked their lives during the fighting. Cárdenas' first significant political position came as governor of his native state from 1928 to 1932. Here he demonstrated that he differed in many ways from the Jefe Máximo. Cárdenas showed himself to be a good listener, making decisions only after soliciting input from all parties. He pursued an aggressive campaign for rural education, opening more than a hundred new schools in remote areas, and he also redistributed some land to campesinos.

Once installed in the presidency, Cárdenas demonstrated that he would direct a much more progressive administration than had his predecessors. He refused to live in Chapultepec Castle and remained in his house in nearby Los Pinos, a house that Calles had once occupied as a member of Obregón's cabinet. When Calles embarked on a six-month trip to Los Angeles to tend to his ailing health, Cárdenas seized the opportunity to build a power base of his own. He supported the workers' right to strike, and within six months of his inauguration, hundreds of workers' organizations had taken advantage of this opportunity. In June 1935, Calles returned from Los Angeles and openly criticized the demonstrations, implying in a message printed in all Mexican newspapers that Cárdenas had lost control of the situation. The president responded by purging his cabinet of all Calles supporters, including the Jefe Máximo's own son, Rodolfo, moves that enjoyed the support of most of Congress. It had become evident that Calles' days at the helm of the revolution were over. On April 9, 1936, Cárdenas gave the Jefe Máximo the choice between prison and exile. His political career finished, Calles took up residence in San Diego.

In control of the revolutionary state and with the economic picture improving in the age of the New Deal in the United States, Cárdenas embarked on an ambitious reform program. He redistributed more than 49 million acres of land to campesinos, or more than twice as much as his revolutionary predecessors combined. His government awarded most of this land to campesinos as ejidos, or communal land, and it organized the campesinos in a new umbrella organization, the Consejo Nacional Campesino (CNC, or National Campesino Council). The ejido structure paid instant dividends in the form of a rapid increase in food production. Cárdenas also took steps to help labor. Under his leadership, the Marxist labor leader Vicente Lombardo Toledano created a new, nationwide labor movement, the Confederación de Trabajadores Mexicanos (CTM, or Confederation of Mexican Workers). Unlike the CROM, which had safeguarded primarily the interests of local labor bosses and its own leader, Morones, the CTM had ideological focus, promising to improve workers' conditions along socialist lines. In many cases, the CTM platform anticipated the later social programs of the Mexican government in the post–World War II period, which featured measures such as subsidized food and housing and nationalization of large businesses. The most significant example of Cárdenas' support for labor came in the case of the foreign-owned oil companies, which had defied labor legislation for many years. Following the companies' refusal to heed a decision of the Mexican Supreme Court favorable to the oil workers, Cárdenas expropriated Standard Oil, Royal Dutch Shell, and fourteen other foreign-owned oil companies on March 18, 1938. This move came only a few weeks after Adolf Hitler's invasion of Austria, when the governments of Great Britain and the United States were more concerned about the Nazi threat than revolutionary nationalism in Mexico. He also took advantage of the friendship of U.S. ambassador Josephus Daniels, who steadfastly defended Mexico's right to make its own laws to his superiors even as the oil companies and Secretary of State Cordell Hull demanded harsh measures against the Cárdenas government. The expropriation found widespread acclaim among the lower and middle classes. For the first time, the Mexican government had seized ownership of an export product. The new national oil company—Petróleos Mexicanos (PEMEX)—was a source of national pride. Finally, Cárdenas became the only president in the Americas to lend assistance to the left-wing Spanish Republicans, locked in a civil war with the Fascist Falange of General Francisco Franco. After Franco's triumph, Cárdenas granted asylum to thousands of Republican refugees from Spain, especially intellectuals and other professionals. These refugees were not only stalwart supporters of Cárdenas, but they also set up Mexico's finest institution of higher learning in the humanities and social sciences, the Colegio de México.

The Cardenista system was a corporatist state in which the president played the role of arbiter of social conflict. Immediately after the oil expropriation, Cárdenas restructured the PNR along corporatist lines. So far, the ruling party had been a confederation of political leaders only. Now the party, renamed Partido de la Revolución Mexicana (PRM, or Party of the Mexican Revolution), included the CNC and the CTM. The new party—and, by extension, President Cárdenas—mediated social conflicts, setting wages and workplace laws and adjudicating conflicts between employers and employees. While workers found many of their goals realized in official policy, they failed to gain the independence in collective bargaining that they wanted. The result of these policies was an increase in the standard of living for many Mexican workers and campesinos at the price of co-opting their organizations into the official party.

Yet the Cárdenas era was not a radical break from the past. Most of the workplace laws came from the Maximato, during which time the government had chosen to ignore the legislation it had approved. Cárdenas' populism also built on the work of his predecessors: the notion that the ruling party represented the revolution, the idea of the revolutionary family, and the rhetoric of economic nationalism. Finally, not all Cardenistas were social revolutionaries, and the president willingly entered into alliances with more conservative political leaders. In Sonora, for instance, Cárdenas had installed a conservative Catholic Mayo Indian in the governor's palace, for the primary reason that the new governor was an archenemy of former Jefe Máximo Calles. Similarly, in Baja California, Nuevo León, and Puebla, governors from wealthy entrepreneur families directed their states. Finally, Cárdenas turned away from reform during his last years in office. After the oil expropriation, the labor leader

Lombardo Toledano lost influence within the national government in favor of Finance Secretary Eduardo Suárez, who advocated capitalist development with safeguards for campesinos and workers. Thus, a significant aspect of the Cárdenas years was the growth of new, privately owned agricultural estates. In Baja California, for example, former president Rodríguez owned newly planted vineyards.

The rise of U.S. influence provided another example of the contradictions of the revolutionary decades in general and the Cárdenas years in particular. To be sure, the oil expropriation had eliminated one particular area of foreign influence in Mexico, and the government had also succeeded in limiting the privileges of foreign residents of Mexico, many of whom had long been able to count on the protection of their embassies in order to obtain preferential treatment by government authorities. In many ways, however, foreign—and particularly United States—influence increased during the 1920s and 1930s. By the end of the Cárdenas administration, foreign investment had actually increased since 1934, especially due to new investments in mining and tourism. In addition, investors discovered the country's growing consumer market as a new opportunity. Industrialization entered a new phase, as Ford Motor Co., Colgate-Palmolive, and many other foreign producers opened plants in Mexico. Even more important was the growth of U.S. cultural influence in an era defined by the coming of mass media, especially radio and motion pictures. Hollywood exported its films south of the border, and Mexicans built cinemas to view them. In turn, Mexico developed its own movie industry, which entered its golden age in the 1940s. Throughout the country, the infrastructural improvements of the preceding decades provided opportunities for the spread of U.S. culture at the same time that they allowed the building of a national one. Thus, consumer culture at last reached many Mexican villages.

The presidential elections of 1940 took place against this backdrop, accompanied by the rumblings of World War II from distant Asia and Europe. In the contest, three generals vied for power, each with a different power base. To Cárdenas' left, Francisco Múgica from Michoacán represented a commitment to ongoing social reform. To his right, Juan Andreu Almazán from Nuevo León enjoyed close ties to the Monterrey industrialists and considerable wealth of his own. Finally, Manuel Avila Camacho from Puebla appeared as the middle-of-the-road candidate. Of the three, Avila Camacho enjoyed the best connections in the form of his brother, Maximino, the strong man of Puebla and one of the wealthiest and most corrupt men in Mexico. On the other hand, Múgica and Almazán found themselves tainted by allegations of cooperation with communists and fascists, respectively. Avila Camacho used his brother's cash as well as the notion that he represented the political center to his advantage and triumphed in the presidential elections.

The election emphasized the threats of World War II, in particular, that of Nazism and Fascism. Foreign observers were worried that Mexico would follow Spain's path into civil war, and they responded with palpable relief when the elections passed without violent incidents. The victorious Avila Camacho immediately portrayed himself as a moderate who would attempt to mend the political divisions of his country. Just a few days after his election, he proclaimed that he was "a believer" in Roman Catholicism in a clear break from his anticlerical predecessors. At a time when the Hitler-Stalin pact conjured up the specter of an alliance of the extreme right and left, he also made it clear that his sympathies lay with the Western Allies. Avila Camacho deposed Lombardo Toledano, the Marxist leader of the CTM labor union and a close friend of Cárdenas. The new labor leader, Fidel Velásquez, had no use for radical ideologies and advocated gradual improvement of wages and benefits. In response to these signs that the Mexican government was swinging back to the right, the U.S. government commenced negotiations that resulted in a settlement of the oil controversy and other pending matters.

This settlement, as well as Hitler's attack on the Soviet Union in June 1941, paved the way for Mexican participation in World War II on the side of the Allies. The day after the Japanese attack on Pearl Harbor on December 7, 1941, Avila Camacho severed diplomatic relations with the Axis powers. Five months later, German submarines sank two Mexican tankers, and the president responded by declaring war on Germany, Italy, and Japan. In spontaneous demonstrations, many Mexicans manifested their support of their government, and in December 1942 Avila Camacho orchestrated a show of national unity, inviting six ex-presidents, including Calles and Cárdenas, to join him at a rally at the Zócalo in Mexico City. Unlike Brazil, Mexico did not send troops to Europe. However, a squadron still remembered by schoolchildren as Escuadrón 201 participated in the fighting in the Pacific theater, and tens of thousands of Mexican immigrants joined the U.S. army.

The war provided a great boost to the Mexican economy. U.S. demand for Mexican raw materials burgeoned, as did the prices for these commodities. The war provided a significant impetus for industrialization. Not only did German U-boat warfare cut Mexico and the rest of Latin America off from trade with Europe, but the United States focused its own industrial production on meeting the needs of the war. As a result, the early 1940s witnessed the beginning of import-substitution industrialization (ISI), a state-sponsored effort to build industries that produced large amounts of manufactured items formerly imported from abroad. ISI would constitute the single most important economic development strategy over the next forty years.

Mexico's participation in World War II marked the end of the revolution. On January 18, 1946, the PRM reformed as the Partido Revolucionario Institucional (PRI, or Institutional Revolutionary Party). The oxymoron was well chosen. The revolution had ended, but it remained alive in the official ideology of the party and its top representative, the president of Mexico. Thus the PRI could point to some real accomplishments of the revolution while deferring the numerous unfinished tasks into the future.

The name change of the party coincided with the passing of the torch to a new generation in the presidential elections of 1946. Carranza, Obregón, Calles, Portes Gil, Rodríguez, Cárdenas, and Avila Camacho had all earned their general's stripes in revolutionary warfare. The new president, Miguel Alemán Valdés, was a college graduate and the son of an army officer who had lost his life in the Escobar Rebellion of 1929. Alemán was just ten years old when Madero raised the specter of revolt against Porfirio Díaz in 1910. His election was uneventful, marking the beginning of a period of more than forty years in which the PRI would govern without a serious electoral challenge. For Alemán, the revolution would remain an official mantra, but the chasm between theory and practice—a familiar theme in Mexican history—became ever more obvious.

The ruins of ancient Chichen Itza. Unless otherwise noted, photographs are by Jürgen Buchenau.

Diego Rivera mural showing his image of Tenochtitlán.

Opposite top: The Sun Pyramid of Teotihuacán.

Opposite bottom: The Aztec Sun Calendar in the Museo de Antropología.

Top: Statue of Cuauhtémoc
in Mexico City.

Bottom: Cathedral in the
Zócalo of Mexico City.

Top: Empress Carlota and Emperor
Maximilian, head-and-shoulders
portraits nestled in flowers, c. 1864.
Library of Congress, LC-USZ62-
17160.

Bottom: Purported to be a photograph
of the execution of Emperor
Maximilian and others by firing squad.
Library of Congress, LC-USZ62-
35351.

Top: Colonial architecture in Alamo, Sonora.

Bottom: Acatepec, the colonial church of Puebla.

General D. Antonio Lopez de Santa Anna, president of the Republic of Mexico, c. 1847. Library of Congress, LC-USZ62-21276.

Porfirio Díaz. Library of Congress, LC-USZ62-22174.

Top: General Pancho Villa and his staff. Library of Congress, LC-DIG-ggbain-29882.

Right: Emilio Zapata. Library of Congress, LC-B2-2915-12[P&P].

Top: Obregón and his staff. Library of Congress, LC-DIG-ggbain-21627.

Bottom: Mexico during the Constitutionalist revolution against Huerta's government. Library of Congress, LC-USZ62-80769.

Opposite top: The church of Arizpe, Sonora, well protected against Apache attacks.

Opposite bottom: The Momument a los Niños Heroes in Mexico City.

Below: Monument to the presidents in Guaymas, Sonora: Adolfo de la Huerta, Plutarco Elías Calles, and Abelardo L. Rodríguez.

Top: The colonial center of Guanajuato

Bottom: A shack near Alamos, Sonora.

Opposite top: Sanborn's Restaurant in La Casa de los Azulejos, a famous colonial building in Mexico City.

Opposite bottom: A street scene in Alamos, Sonora.

UNAM, Mexico City.

Opposite top: Day of the Dead altar.

Opposite bottom: BBQ stand in Mexico state.

Landscape near Arizpe, Sonora.

CHAPTER FIVE

❧ Mexico since World War II ☙

September 11, 1971, was show time in Avándaro. At least 250,000 rock fans had congregated in this picturesque town two hours west of the capital to celebrate a Mexican version of Woodstock—a weekend of *rocanrol* and slumming in tents. Almost all of them were young, many of them students, and most of them from the capital and other large cities. Held near the location of a car race, the event was just as muddy as the original rock festival held in upstate New York after a torrential rainfall. Like Woodstock, Avándaro amounted to a respite from social conservatism, featuring plenty of bad language, drug and alcohol use, and sex. And like that of Woodstock, the urban clientele of the Avándaro festival contrasted with a local rural culture uninterested in rock music, albeit one thoroughly immersed in the project of national economic development. Just minutes away, the tourist town of Valle del Bravo offered a bucolic escape that advertised itself to tourists with its traditional culture. In Valle del Bravo, artisans sold hand-woven baskets and shawls, and traditional bands played "Las Mañanitas" and revolutionary corridos.

Yet Avándaro differed from Woodstock in significant ways. The festival took place under the threat of government repression. Three years before, government forces had massacred hundreds of student protesters at Tlatelolco, a suburb of Mexico City, and the massacre had created an underground radical opposition movement. With its sexually and politically explicit lyrics, rock music challenged dominant social values such as patriarchy and submission to authority. At Avándaro, a youth culture quashed by the force of guns at Tlatelolco reared its head once again. As a result, television and radio stations assiduously ignored the event, and to this day, many Mexicans have never heard of it. Even more amazing, the record industry did not profit from the event. Unlike Woodstock, which greatly boosted sales of recorded rock music, Avándaro resulted in no such windfall for its artists, as the Mexican music industry did not release records by the bands that played at the festival.

The rock festival illustrated significant tensions that characterize modern Mexico: between cosmopolitan and local cultures, between students and their parents, between urban and rural Mexicans, and between those aspiring for democracy and those holding onto the legacy of authoritarian rule. Avándaro highlights the impact of globalization on postwar Mexico, and the ways in which Mexicans have attempted to shape these global influences to fit their own culture. As the cultural critic Carlos Monsiváis stated: "The Mexican assimilates without being assimilated." Indeed, rocanrol was not a carbon copy of Anglophone rock music, and it never became the craze that has sustained a multimillion dollar industry in North America and Western Europe. But over the coming decades, Mexico did become a major producer of commercialized mass culture in the form of the telenovela. Both rock music and soap operas are examples of the cultural and commercial interplay with the outside world that has increasingly defined Mexican society in a global age. In recent decades, global trends have helped Mexicans undermine the hegemony of the PRI—a party that claimed its legitimacy from a nationalist revolution.

THE HEYDAY OF THE PRI AND THE "MEXICAN MIRACLE," 1946–1968

The most significant plank of the platform of the Partido Revolucionario Institucional was that of state-sponsored national economic development. This strategy sought to combine the advantages of liberal capitalism with the benefits of state economic planning. At a time when the Cold War divided much of the world, pitting a capitalist camp under the leadership of the United States against the communist Soviet Union and its allies, the PRI professed to embrace a middle position that took advantage of the best aspects of both economic philosophies. In fact, however, the PRI's development model firmly hitched itself to the capitalist economies of the West, while giving the state an important role to play in the promotion of industrialization. Taking advantage of favorable conditions, the PRI-led state oversaw decades of rapid economic growth, a phenomenon that the party's leadership dubbed the "Mexican miracle." Between 1950 and 1973, the per capita domestic product doubled in real terms.

The economic growth of this period followed a brief but severe economic crisis in the immediate postwar years. World War II had greatly benefited

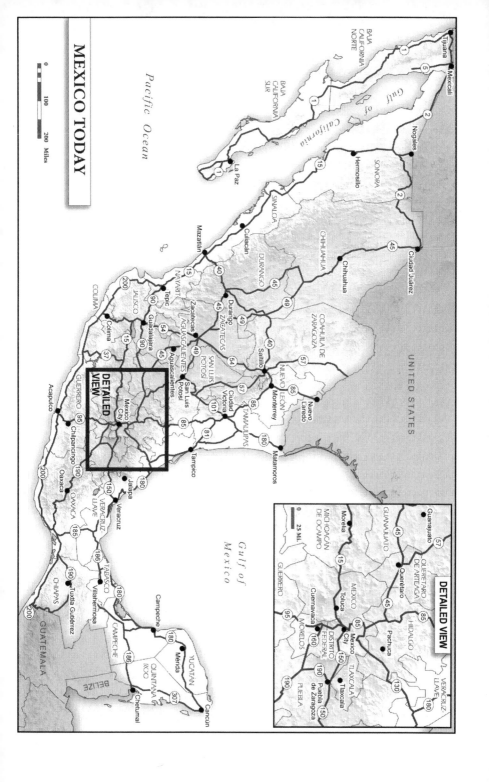

the Mexican economy, as Mexico had helped the Allied war effort in large part by furnishing such strategic raw materials as metals and minerals. The postwar drop in demand for these products hurt the Mexican economy severely. When the end of the war removed a major stimulus for the U.S. economy, U.S. businesses also sent home tens of thousands of Mexican *braceros*, guestworkers hired during the war, adding pressure to a labor market already straining under the weight of a growing population. At the same time, mounting inflation, particularly in foodstuffs and other necessary items, confounded the expectations of many Mexicans that the Allied victory in the war would benefit them.

Faced with this reality, the Mexican government joined other large Latin American nations in embracing the advice of the Argentine economist Raúl Prebisch, the president of the United Nations' Economic Commission for Latin America. Along with other large Latin American nations such as Argentina and Brazil, the Mexican government had discovered the benefits of "import-substitution industrialization" (ISI) during World War II, a time during which it could not depend on the importation of manufactured products. At the time, the government had begun discussions about protecting its industries—those that produced textiles, glass, hardware, and other component products—by means of imposing tariffs on imported manufactured items. Prebisch went a step further and diagnosed the reliance on externally driven development—the export of raw materials to pay for imported industrial goods—as the cause for the economic underdevelopment of Latin America. According to Prebisch's analysis, trading raw materials for manufactured products constituted an "unequal exchange," as the prices of most raw materials tended to decline in the long run in comparison to those of manufactured goods. To solve this problem, Prebisch proposed government-assisted ISI programs accompanied by a protectionist trade policy. Picking up on an industrialization project that had brought many industries to Mexico over the course of the preceding sixty years—such as steel, beer, and chemicals—the Mexican government made a strong push toward state-assisted modernization. Domestic industries could count on the protection of the government, which imposed punitive tariffs on imports that competed with their products. Of course, the success of this plan depended on foreign demand for Mexican raw materials. Fortunately, strong economic growth in the United States and the postwar recovery of Western Europe created such a demand, plus a growing tourist industry as well as increasing remittances from Mexican workers in the United States poured cash into the Mexican economy.

The ISI effort did not imply a move toward true economic independence—an impossible endeavor in any case. Rather, it changed the nature of

Mexico's dependence on the United States and, to a lesser extent, western Europe. Instead of buying hardware abroad, for example, Mexican companies purchased the machinery needed to produce such hardware. Another development was the opening in Mexico of foreign-owned assembly plants during the 1950s and 1960s, which followed a trend begun before the war. For example, in 1966 Volkswagen began to produce its signature Beetle automobile in its new plant in the city of Puebla, and dozens of large U.S. corporations including General Motors, Dow Chemicals, Coca-Cola, Ford, and Goodyear invested in Mexico. Financed in part by government subsidies, *maquiladoras*, or partial assembly plants, dotted the northern states close to the U.S. border, from where the maquiladoras shipped their products to be fully finished in the United States. The stimulation of the maquiladora industry formed part of the government's response to the return of the braceros after World War II, but it was also an effort to develop Mexico's border region further.

In light of Mexico's ever-closer economic relationship with the United States, the ongoing "Americanization" of Mexican living habits infiltrated popular culture. For example, Mexicans discovered hamburgers and Coke. Their consumption of fizzy beverages permeated so deeply in Mexican society that the United States and Mexico have taken turns leading the world in per-capita consumption of soft drinks. Even in remote villages that do not have electricity, let alone Internet access, Coke and other sodas are available. Mexicans also discovered television, the national pastime of the United States. By the 1970s, Mexican studios produced a variety of soap operas—shows so popular that they were exported to other Latin American countries. Finally, U.S.-style shopping came to Mexico in the form of Sears-Roebuck, which opened its first department store at the busy Avenida Insurgentes in Mexico City in 1947. A few decades thereafter, many inhabitants of the capital would abandon their traditional shopping trip to the historic city center in favor of driving to one of the brand-new, U.S.-style shopping malls, complete with food courts, movie theaters, and ample parking.

Americanization also arrived in the form of mass tourism, a sector that became one of the mainstays of the economy. Mexico has had a long history as a tourist destination. During the late 1910s and 1920s, thousands of U.S. citizens had sought refuge there from the rigid laws of the Prohibition era in the brothels, bars, and casinos of the border state of Baja California. At the same time, Mexico became a temporary home for cultural pilgrims, left-leaning foreign visitors who wanted to view the revolution up close. Particularly important among those cultural pilgrims was Frank Tannenbaum, a historian who applauded the PRI's development model and advertised it in the United

States. Tannenbaum's publications and the improving relations between the United States and Mexico during World War II set the stage for a tourist boom during the ensuing decades. Once a quaint town on a perfect, crescent-shaped beach, Acapulco became the first tourist magnet of the 1950s until its rapid growth destroyed the environment and blunted much of its attraction. Afterward, tourists in search of sand and sun discovered other resort towns along the Pacific such as Puerto Vallarta in Jalisco, Zihuatanejo in Guerrero, and Puerto Escondido in Oaxaca. Other foreign visitors flocked to the country's cultural treasures. San Miguel de Allende, a beautiful colonial town in the state of Guanajuato, became a favorite spot for U.S. and Canadian retirees. Also, the Mexican government advertised the country's pre-Columbian and colonial past to a U.S. and European audience. Teotihuacán near Mexico City and the Maya sites of Chichén Itzá, Uxmal, and Palenque became major tourist destinations, as did the colonial towns of Cuernavaca, Guanajuato, Puebla, and Oaxaca. Glossy magazines advertised these sites as places where visitors could forget the modern world and lose themselves in the past, even though the new hotels near the archaeological and colonial sites boasted modern amenities such as air conditioning, sumptuous meals, and imported beverages.

With the help of strong U.S. demand for Mexican products, ISI produced results that looked impressive. At an average annual rate, the GNP grew 8 percent in the 1948–68 period, accompanied by great strides in literacy and health care. Illiteracy had remained as high as 70 percent during the Great Depression; by 1960, however, almost 80 percent of adult Mexicans enjoyed some degree of functional literacy. Finally, the country's road system reached all corners of the republic: the 1960s witnessed the completion of the road from Veracruz to Campeche, the first link of the Yucatán peninsula to the rest of the nation. Many observers considered the country one of the newly industrializing nations along with Japan, South Korea, and Taiwan.

The comparisons to those three East Asian nations proved exaggerated, as Mexico's economic performance was impressive in Latin American but not in global terms. The country with the leading economy in Latin America on a per capita basis, Argentina outpaced Mexico during the heyday of Peronism (1946–52), only to fall back dramatically as the effects of Juan and Evita Perón's enormous spending took their toll. The economy of Mexico, however, lagged behind those of the United States and Western Europe, particularly when adjusted for population. The economies of Hong Kong, Japan, South Korea, and Taiwan all outpaced that of Mexico based on a similar economic paradigm.

Finally, the ISI model brought Mexico a new set of social problems in the form of runaway urbanization. Beginning with the Alemán administration, the PRI bureaucrats abandoned their efforts to help alleviate rural poverty, and millions of campesinos fled to the cities in search of a better life. The result was a more urban society: metropolitan Mexico City grew from 650,000 inhabitants in 1945 to 20 million forty years later, and other urban centers such as Guadalajara, León, Monterrey, and Puebla also experienced exponential growth. Much of this growth attested to the fact that poverty was on the rise even as national income improved, as a ring of *ciudades perdidas* (lost cities), or shantytowns, came to surround Mexico City and other metropolitan areas. Most of the ciudades perdidas were makeshift settlements of poor migrants who used leftover construction supplies, wood, and cardboard to build their leaky shacks. Rampant crime, abject poverty, and the absence of sewerage systems and running water made the ciudades perdidas into the flip side of the Mexican miracle. Yet even under these conditions, the Mexican people's urge to survive prevailed, and over time, new social hierarchies and economic opportunities emerged. By the mid-1980s, the largest of the shantytowns, Ciudad Nezahualcóyotl just east of Mexico City, had 3 million inhabitants and was the home of a small but growing middle sector that settled in "Neza," as its inhabitants call their city, to escape the high rent and cost of living in the national capital. Today, Neza boasts paved streets, electric lighting, and a soccer stadium large and modern enough to be was chosen as one of the sites of the 1986 soccer World Cup, held in Mexico after Colombia had shown itself unable to host the event.

The emergence of shantytowns such as Neza was only one aspect of a larger process of migration on a massive scale. The postwar decades witnessed a surge in Mexican immigration to the United States. Mexicans crossed the border lured by the availability of jobs in farming and construction and immigration legislation that (at least until the early 1970s) waived restrictions on American nations. They joined other Latino immigrants such as Dominicans, Puerto Ricans, and Cubans in transforming U.S. society. While Caribbean immigrants flocked to Florida and large cities in the Northeast and Midwest such as New York, Boston, and Chicago, most Mexicans settled in the area that had once belonged to their nation, the U.S. Southwest. In California, Arizona, New Mexico, and Texas, the Chicano population ascended to millions. For their part, U.S. employers relished the opportunity to hire foreign workers at less than the customary wages paid American laborers. The burgeoning Mexican population in the United States led to the emergence of movements to defend the interests of immigrant labor. Most important among those was the National Farm Workers Association (later, the United Farm Workers) under the leadership of César Estrada Chávez. The presence of a large Mexican population in the United States also encouraged the cross-fertilization of both cultures:

just as Los Angelenos came to appreciate enchiladas and tacos, braceros and other Mexicans returning to their homeland introduced their peers to football and North American rock music.

The economic "Mexican miracle" followed the golden age of Mexican entertainment, particularly with regard to popular music and cinema. Mass culture had finally succeeded in what politicians had thus far failed to do: promote a national consciousness based on a shared culture. One example of the enormous popularity of an entertainment star is Pedro Infante, perhaps the most famous Mexican singer and actor of his age. Beginning in 1939, he recorded more than 350 songs and appeared in more than 60 films. Through his various roles, he represented the "average" Mexican, whether as a rural *charro*, or cowboy, or as a member of the urban working class. A fun-loving womanizer fond of parties, Infante personified a caricature of a Mexican. Much like James Dean in the United States, tragedy elevated him to iconic stature when he died in a plane crash in 1957 at the age of thirty-nine. More than 150,000 people attended Infante's funeral, and according to historian Anne Rubenstein, his popularity is still legendary, so that many Mexicans professed as recently as 1998 that Infante faked his own death in order to escape the public spotlight. Another example of a cultural icon is María Félix (1914–2002), the daughter of a Yaqui father and a Spanish mother. Rumored to be President Miguel Alemán's mistress, and in fact the partner of singer Agustín Lara, Félix was a diva whose popularity transcended traditional morals. Probably the most important star of the golden age of Mexican cinema, however, was Fortino Mario Alfonso Moreno Reyes (1911–93), a man most Mexicans knew only as his character, Cantinflas. Dubbed the "Charlie Chaplin of Mexico" by U.S. observers, Reyes was a comedian whose stock character was the *pelado*, or hapless member of the "uncultured" urban poor. Cantinflas became a spokesperson for the less fortunate and even the illiterate. Like Infante, he epitomized "Mexicanness" in a popular rather than elite manifestation. In the words of historian Jeffrey Pilcher, Cantinflas "symbolized the underdog who triumphed through trickery over more powerful opponents." All three of these examples of popular stars demonstrate the extent to which cultural representations in film and song redefined *mexicanidad* along lines quite different from the views of the PRI, whose slogans claimed that all Mexicans faced a prosperous future under the party's leadership. Infante, Félix, and Reyes all played to the more cynical attitude held by the majority of people who knew everyday life to be a struggle for survival. At the same time, these actors allowed ordinary Mexicans to transcend the social realities of their own lives by means of humor.

At this time, the ruling party's authority began to erode in other ways as well. It had become increasingly apparent that the PRI could no longer claim to be the custodian of the Mexican Revolution. And a party that advertised itself as a nationalist defender of its country's sovereignty proudly remembered Cárdenas's oil expropriation of 1938 but meekly allowed foreigners to grab a significant share of the tourist industry—one of the most rapidly growing sectors of the economy. And while the PRI proclaimed its allegiance to land reform and workers' rights, the party quietly ended its support for further land redistributions and encouraged CTM leader Fidel Velásquez to strike a cooperative stance with business leaders and to expel communist leaders from the labor union. Ultimately, democracy remained an elusive dream in Mexico, as the PRI dominated politics at the national, state, and local levels. The political opposition, led by the conservative Partido Acción Nacional (PAN, or National Action Party), did not win any offices of consequence until the late 1980s. The only major improvement in the political arena during this time was President Adolfo Ruiz Cortines's institution of women's suffrage in 1953, an amendment first proposed under Cárdenas. Five years later, women turned out in large numbers at their first opportunity to cast ballots in a presidential election. Nevertheless the outcome was the same: the easy triumph of the PRI candidate, in this case Adolfo López Mateos. Indeed, the victory of the PRI was so automatic throughout the period 1946–88 that most observers focused on another event as being the decisive one in the campaign: the party's unveiling of its candidate for president. In reality, as Mexicans knew, each sitting president chose his own successor: hence, as mentioned, the nomination of the next PRI presidential candidate became known as the dedazo, or finger point.

For those Mexicans who were disappointed in the institutionalized revolution in their own country, the triumph of the Cuban Revolution on New Years Day, 1959, was significant to them. The victory of Fidel Castro, Che Guevara, and their allies ushered in the second major social revolution in Latin America, one far more radical and ideologically unified than Mexico's great upheaval earlier in the twentieth century. A little more than a month after their triumph, a number of bearded Cuban revolutionaries visited Mexico to widespread acclaim. At that point, no one knew what to expect of the Cuban Revolution. Over the next two years, however, an escalating conflict between the revolutionaries and the U.S. government led to the wholesale nationalization of U.S. property in Cuba, the rupture of diplomatic relations between the two nations, and the establishment of a communist government in Cuba allied with the Soviet Union. While few Mexicans advocated the establishment of a similarly radical government, many people critical of the PRI regarded Castro's Cuba as an alternate revolutionary model with many praiseworthy aspects. They admired Castro's steadfast refusal to compromise with the United States and his rhetoric calling for social justice and true independence from imperialist powers.

President López Mateos recognized the symbolic power of the Cuban Revolution in Mexico. He knew that Castro's triumph reminded Mexicans that the PRI had stalled the momentum of its own revolution. Former labor leader Vicente Lombardo Toledano immediately seized the opportunity of the Cuban visit to encourage a railroad strike in March 1959. This strike, although quickly crushed by police, showed López Mateos the strength of the organized left, both within and outside of the PRI. Even former president Cárdenas openly showed his sympathies with the Cuban Revolution. When a U.S.-sponsored expedition invaded Cuba at the Bay of Pigs in April 1961, Cárdenas offered to travel to Cuba to help Castro defeat the invaders. As a result, López Mateos sought to earn political capital by expressing lukewarm support of the Castro government until the complete breakdown of U.S.-Cuban relations in early 1961 made such a stance impossible. He defended the Cuban Revolution both against the United States and against conservatives within his own country, who matched public demonstrations in favor of Castro with their own anticommunist gatherings. In June 1960, he even hosted Cuban president Osvaldo Dorticós, the first Cuban head of state to visit Mexico. During the visit, the Mexican president declared: "We, who have gone through similar stages, understand and value the Cuban effort at transformation. . . . We hope that the Cuban Revolution might be, like ours has been, another step toward [achieving] the greatness of America." But later, for fear of U.S. reprisals after the failed Bay of Pigs invasion, López Mateos shifted toward only an abstract defense of Cuba's right to choose its own political system.

López Mateos's defense of the right to national self-determination in Cuba followed an old tradition in Mexican diplomacy—a tradition borne out of Mexico's own painful experiences with foreign intervention. But it also responded to the growing popular criticism of the PRI. Protesters not only resisted the entrenchment of the PRI as Mexico's ruling party, but also the party's abandonment of the principles under which it had been founded. One example of the protest movements was that of the agrarian rebel Rubén Jaramillo from Morelos, who considered himself Zapata's heir in fighting for land reform. Jaramillo commanded a small guerrilla force in Morelos until 1958, when the Mexican government offered the guerillas amnesty in return for laying down their arms. As mentioned above, López Mateos brutally suppressed a railroad workers' strike demanding better wages and benefits, and in May 1962 the judicial police imprisoned and massacred Jaramillo along with his wife and three children. In other states such as Guerrero, Oaxaca, and Puebla, teachers' protest movements called for municipal autonomy, democracy, and social justice.

Mexicans proudly anticipated October 1968, when their capital hosted the first Olympic Games ever awarded to a developing nation. The successful Olympic bid appeared to validate the ISI development strategy, and the PRI leadership advertised its role in making Mexico into a modern nation that was flush enough to host one of the world's two premier sporting events. The other, as mentioned, was the soccer World Cup, scheduled to be held in Mexico two years later—an even greater accomplishment, given the wild popularity of the sport throughout Europe and Latin America. As President Gustavo Díaz Ordaz put it, Mexico had arrived among the most advanced nations of the world.

Yet the preparations for the Olympics turned sour. The year 1968 marked the beginning of radical student protests in France, Germany, Mexico, and the United States. Although the Vietnam War was one catalyst for the protests around the world, student protestors in Mexico City had primarily domestic issues in mind. They used the global spotlight of the Olympics as an opportunity to press demands for a more just and democratic society. In particular, students demanded the release of all political prisoners, the firing of a police chief known for his ruthless brutality, and the dissolution of the *granaderos*, or paramilitary riot police. Incensed at what he viewed as a lack of gratitude and respect by the university students, President Díaz Ordaz met their demands with repression, and his government's response to the student movement was far more drastic than that of authorities in other nations. On August 27, half a million people demonstrated peacefully on the Zócalo of Mexico City. As the rally continued past nightfall, army tanks moved into the area to break up the demonstration, and one student died during the ensuing violence. Less than three weeks later, 10,000 army troops occupied the campus of the National University and arrested hundreds of students to discourage further demonstrations. The bloody denouement of the student protest occurred on October 2, 1968, when approximately 5,000 protesters assembled at the Plaza de las Tres Culturas in Tlatelolco, Mexico City. Early that evening, the army sent armored cars and tanks, using loudspeakers to order the crowd to disperse. When the protesters did not comply, the government forces began firing, and pandemonium ensued. The official version of the events was that snipers in nearby buildings had opened fire on the police and army forces, while surviving protesters claimed that the government's men opened fire unprovoked with automatic weapons. Although the order of the events at Tlatelolco has never been settled conclusively, the available evidence indicates that the Díaz Ordaz government was responsible for the death of more than four hundred protesters. A few weeks later, the Olympics went off without a hitch. But the quiet city that greeted thousands of visitors from the rest of the world now had the ambience of a morgue.

THE CRISIS OF THE POSTREVOLUTIONARY MODEL, 1968–1988

The Tlatelolco massacre ushered in a long political and social crisis and de-stroyed whatever credibility the notion of the institutional revolution still held. At the Plaza de las Tres Culturas, the government's guns had mowed down peaceful protesters who had dared to remind the regime of its promises for a more just and democratic society. Rather than recalling the struggles of Zapata or the battles of Villa and Obregón, the Tlatelolco massacre reminded Mexi-cans of the bloody suppression of the Cananea and Río Blanco strikes in the waning years of the Porfiriato. Unlike the two earlier cases, however, the 1968 massacre had felled young members of the urban middle class. This class had materially benefited from the economic boom of the preceding decades, but the student protesters and many of their parents now felt that the increasingly authoritarian PRI, as the supposed heir of the revolution, had failed them in its betrayal of its own principles.

Stung by the widespread public outrage about Tlatelolco, Luis Echeverría Alvarez, the party's candidate for president in 1970, pursued a twofold strategy of reform and repression. On the one hand, Echeverría fashioned himself as the most progressive Mexican president since Cárdenas, a champion of the poor and an advocate of the interests of underdeveloped nations in general. He revived the land distribution program, parceling out more acres than had any president since Cárdenas; he launched ambitious social and public works programs funded by the state; and he imposed a luxury tax on expensive pur-chases. Like don Porfirio, Echeverría co-opted members of the opposition into his government, thus casting himself as a conciliatory and unifying leader. The president also portrayed himself as a champion of the so-called Third World. He railed against U.S. policies in Chile, Cuba, and the Middle East, posing for photo opportunities with Cuban socialist leader Fidel Castro and the Palestin-ian leader Yasser Arafat. In 1974, the discovery of huge offshore oil reserves in the Gulf of Mexico, coupled with an oil price spike in the aftermath of the Yom Kippur War, further emboldened Echeverría. When a military coup overthrew Chile's democratically elected socialist government under President Salvador Allende, who died in the process, the president invited thousands of refugees, including Allende's widow, to accept exile in Mexico.

On the other hand, Echeverría brutally cracked down on the protest movement. At the same time that he advertised Mexico as a haven for refugees from right-wing dictatorships in South and Central America, he pursued an unyielding campaign against the left at home. Although in 1971 Echeverría released most of the students imprisoned in the months and weeks leading up to the Olympics, he crushed those opponents who had remained at large and built up clandestine resistance movements. Some of these movements, including the Movimiento Armado Revolucionario (MAR, or Armed Revolutionary Movement), carried out violent crimes, including bank robberies, kidnappings, and murders, such as the killing of Monterrey industrialist Eugenio Garza Sada. In rural Guerrero, Lucio Cabañas and Genaro Vázquez led small guerrilla forces that kidnapped the federal senator from that state, the PRI candidate for governor. In 1974, both rebel leaders were killed during skirmishes with the army. But President Echeverría targeted innocent civilians as well as those who committed crimes. During his six-year tenure, his war against the left claimed at least six hundred lives, in all likelihood more than the Brazilian dictatorship in its twenty years of existence from 1964 to 1984.

Mexicans might have forgiven Echeverría for his duplicitous political stance if the economy had continued its strong performance from the 1950s and 1960s. However, the dynamic that had sustained the so-called miracle unraveled during the Echeverría years. Government spending and worldwide inflation contributed to an increase in consumer prices by more than 40 percent between January 1973 and December 1974. Less than two years later, the peso lost 50 percent of its value to the U.S. dollar in the first devaluation since 1954. Inflation and devaluation eroded the purchasing power of the very groups who had benefited most from the economic expansion of the past twenty years: middle-class professionals, owners of small and midsized farms, and workers earning more than the minimum wage. At the same time, corruption in the government reached new heights. For example, PEMEX officials sold an estimated 10 percent of oil produced for their personal gain.

What was most problematic for Echeverría and the PRI was that repression, economic crisis, and corruption further highlighted the emptiness of the party's revolutionary rhetoric. It had become clear that the PRI had become an institution devoted principally to prolonging its own power rather than furthering the ideals embodied in the revolutionary Constitution of 1917. Intellectuals studied the body politic and asked rhetorically: "Is the Mexican Revolution dead?" By 1976, most observers answered in the affirmative, and to some, the PRI state resembled its Porfirian predecessor in its emphasis on political order at the expense of human rights and social justice.

Echeverría's successor, José López Portillo, attempted to get the PRI back on track. He used the newly discovered oil reserves as collateral to borrow billions of dollars from foreign banks, rekindling Echeverría's social programs and driving up domestic spending and consumption. Unfortunately, his borrowing occurred at a time of high interest rates and soaring inflation worldwide, resulting in double-digit returns for banks willing to loan money. Over time, the mounting debt put pressure on the peso, but López Portillo reassured nervous Mexicans that he would "defend the peso like a dog." Tourism also got a great boost, as evidenced by the building of the country's largest resort, Cancún, located off the northeastern tip of the peninsula of Yucatán. The development of Cancún inaugurated tremendous economic growth on the Caribbean coast and the development of other lucrative tourist zones on the island of Cozumel and farther south in locations such as Playa del Carmen and Tulum.

López Portillo also continued his predecessor's activist foreign policy, but with a new twist. Whereas Echeverría tried to be a global political player, the new president focused his energies on nearby Central America. In July 1979, the fall of the brutal and corrupt Nicaraguan dictator Anastasio Somoza gave López Portillo the opportunity to help a new regime born out of a social revolution, the Sandinista junta, which arrived in the capital of Managua aboard a Mexican airliner. Over the next two years, the Mexican government provided the socialist Sandinistas with loans, oil, and technology, and in 1981 López Portillo went one step further when he joined French President François Mitterrand in a resolution designed to help another group of socialist revolutionaries in El Salvador gain international standing.

But, like Echeverría's administration, that of López Portillo ended in disappointment and scandal. In 1981, U.S. president Ronald Reagan claimed that both the Sandinistas and the Salvadoran rebels were lackeys of Cuba and the Soviet Union, and on this rationale he sent military assistance to the repressive Salvadoran military and a Nicaraguan opposition group that included several high-ranking Somoza supporters. Even worse, López Portillo had over-borrowed and overspent. In 1982, Mexico defaulted on its foreign loans, and the peso lost more than 85 percent of its value. As cynical Mexicans saw it, the López Portillo administration had landed in the doghouse, a victim of its own false promises and reassurances. The real consequences of the debt crisis were no joking matter. The ensuing hyperinflation cut real wages in half, impoverished millions of workers, and led to a massive capital flight as both foreign and Mexican investors moved billions of dollars out of Mexico. In response, López Portillo nationalized Mexico's banks, further compounding the crisis and driving away foreign investment. Mexico was at the mercy of its creditors at a moment when its president found himself at loggerheads with the right-wing U.S. administration over its support of a socialist government in Nicaragua. As if that were not enough, the president and his associates spent their last months in office enriching themselves and thus draining the national treasury of much of what was left.

The collapse of 1982 constituted the most serious economic and political crisis of postwar Mexican history. If the Tlatelolco massacre had unmasked the PRI as a repressive party that lived on the slogans of yesteryear, the debt crisis revealed the bankruptcy of the party's developmental model. The collapse finished off the PRI's credibility with regard to the national economy, as the International Monetary Fund (IMF) imposed a severe austerity package on the Mexican government as a condition for new loans to bring the country back from default. The austerity package forced new president Miguel de la Madrid Hurtado, a lawyer with a degree in Public Administration from Harvard University, to implement drastic cuts in social programs, including significant reductions in government subsidies for rent and food staples such as rice, beans, and tortillas. The cuts hit Mexican workers and the middle class hard, as both groups had just lost a significant portion of their real wages to inflation. Worse yet, both inflation and devaluation of the peso continued at a breakneck pace. According to official figures, inflation approached 64 percent in 1985 and 159 percent two years later. The peso, which had stood at 25 to the dollar before the debt crisis, fell from 150 to the dollar at the date of de la Madrid's inauguration to 2,300 to the dollar in the summer of 1987, marking a decline of almost 99 percent since 1982. Unemployment also soared, reaching 25 percent in the middle of the decade. Predictably, employee pay could not keep pace, and real wages declined by at least 40 percent between 1983 and 1988. For these reasons, Mexicans referred to the 1980s as the "lost decade."

The long economic crisis, a decline from which Mexicans have never truly recovered, added to the flood of migrants headed north of the border. By 2002, the U.S. census data estimated the number of its population of Mexican origin to be 25 million, and many of the latest arrivals bypassed the Southwest—the traditional locus of Mexican immigration—in favor of new destinations where jobs were available. For example, the Mexican population of Charlotte, North Carolina, numbered several hundred in 1980; twenty-five years later, unofficial estimates in this booming New South metropolitan area ran as high as 40,000.

De la Madrid's answer to this crisis was to embrace neoliberalism, an updated version of the nineteenth-century Liberal emphasis on private initiative rather than state economic planning. Conceived by the University of Chicago economist Milton Friedman, neoliberalism challenged core elements of Mexico's development model since the Cárdenas administration, such as a progressive tax structure, protectionist tariffs and import regulations, price and currency controls, and high spending on social services. Neoliberalism also advocated the creation of international trade agreements to reduce tariffs on a reciprocal basis. In the short run, Mexican neoliberals called for the privatization of the many state-owned enterprises such as Telmex, the national telephone company, and PEMEX. As a PEMEX employee during the early 1970s, de la Madrid had witnessed the corrupt bureaucracy of the state-owned corporations during the very worst period in their history. Privatization not only offered opportunities for private investment, but by selling off state assets, the government tapped into a much-needed source of cash for a national treasury that remained depleted throughout the 1980s. Between 1983 and 1988, the administration sold off 40 percent of the more than 1,000 state-owned companies, though not PEMEX, an icon of nationalism associated in the minds of many Mexicans with the heroic Cárdenas years. In yet another illustration of the wide chasm between rhetoric and practice, in 1988 the government issued a coin commemorating the fiftieth anniversary of the oil expropriation, an ironic choice of motif in an era of privatization. In the end, de la Madrid was far more popular abroad than at home. Mexicans, who had just had a taste of IMF-prescribed austerity, found neoliberalism to be a bitter medicine that eliminated many of the state-funded benefits that had helped sustain the PRI in power for so long. For example, de la Madrid further cut down on housing and food subsidies, reduced the salaries of thousands of government employees, and eliminated 51,000 federal government jobs.

Perhaps the signal event of the de la Madrid era occurred on September 19, 1985. At 7:19 A.M. local time that day, a devastating earthquake shook Mexico City and its environs, measuring 8.1 on the Richter scale. According to official statistics, the quake lasted almost four minutes, killed more than 9,000 people, injured approximately 30,000, and left at least 100,000 homeless. Many observers, however, claimed that the true figures were much higher. Of course, no one in the government could have prevented the disaster. But the earthquake revealed that Mexico had deeper problems than the human death toll and property damage. For example, the collapse of two tall buildings in a housing development near the Plaza de las Tres Culturas in Tlatelolco—the site of the 1968 massacre of student protesters—revealed the extent of government corruption. An examination of the rubble revealed that the buildings were not built to meet structural standards in force at the time of construction even though the plans for the housing development had strictly adhered to and even exceeded that standard. It became obvious to residents that contractors had colluded with government officials to build cheaper, less sturdy buildings, splitting the savings with these officials for personal benefit. In addition, the government's emergency response left much to be desired. Its inability or unwillingness to meet the needs of earthquake victims added to the already widespread sense among Mexico City residents that the PRI had abandoned them. Like the 1968 massacre and the repression of the 1970s, the response to the 1985 earthquake served as a cynical reminder of the corruption within the political system in general and the PRI in particular. As the 1980s—a time Mexicans recall as the "lost decade"—continued, many began to look for a political alternative.

MEXICO IN TRANSITION, 1988–PRESENT

The 1988 elections that were to choose a successor to de la Madrid therefore found the PRI leadership at a crossroads. For years the party had used its control of the federal government to maintain its hold on power. Elections were supervised by a federal institution closely tied to PRI circles, and only the ruling party was able to use the national colors during each electoral campaign. Under the guise of enabling illiterate citizens to cast votes, election officials designed a ballot that prominently displayed the colors and emblem of each party. Thus in 1988, citizens could vote for the PRI candidate, the Harvard-trained technocrat Carlos Salinas de Gortari, by marking through a large square containing the letters PRI within a red, white, and green circle (the colors of the Mexican flag). Or, they could vote for Rafael Clouthier, candidate of the conservative PAN, by marking a square with the blue and white logo of that party. Clouthier enjoyed the support of much of the middle class, particularly in the north and center. That year, citizens had yet another choice for president, a most intriguing one: Cuauhtémoc Cárdenas, the son of the most beloved president of revolutionary Mexico, who had broken with the PRI over de la Madrid's neoliberal policies and the PRI-endorsed electoral process. Cárdenas ran as the candidate of the recently formed Frente Democrático Nacional (FDN, or National Democratic Front), the precursor of the present-day Partido de la Revolución Democrática, or Party of the Democratic Revolution (PRD). The colors of Cárdenas's movement were yellow and black, and his support came primarily from the lower classes as well as educated professionals with progressive leanings. Clearly the exclusive use of the national colors gave the PRI an advantage in this and all other elections.

Although one might have expected another easy triumph for the PRI, the election of 1988 marked the end of its hegemony. On election eve, after the polls had closed, early returns indicated that Cárdenas was headed for an upset victory. All of a sudden, however, a mysterious "crash" of the electoral computer system halted the count. By the time the system went back online a week later, Cárdenas's advantage had disappeared, and the government announced that Salinas had been elected president with 50.7 percent of the vote—the smallest margin of victory in any presidential election since the Restored Republic. The opposition (PAN and FDN) won 48 percent of all seats in the Chamber of Deputies, the lower house of Congress, and enjoyed the power to block any amendments to the constitution. The partisans of the FDN alleged fraud, but to no avail. On December 1, 1988, Salinas took office with the lowest official vote total for a PRI candidate to date.

However, Salinas soon found out that he could count on the conservative PAN to carry out the neoliberal reform program he envisioned. Salinas was the first Mexican president to hold a doctorate conferred abroad, and his style of rule recalled the old Porfirian dictum "more administration, less politics." Like de la Madrid, he desired to privatize state-owned businesses, to liberalize foreign trade, and to give free rein to private investors. But he intended to go one step further by striking nationalist and social reformist provisions from the 1917 constitution. In his words, his administration proposed to "reform the Revolution." Salinas likened his neoliberal policies to Mikhail Gorbachev's *perestroika* in the Soviet Union, a restructuring of a communist economy along capitalist lines. Of course, the parallel was misleading, as Mexico, unlike the Soviet Union, had never left the path of state-sponsored capitalism. Salinas sold off more than 1,000 state-owned companies, the most notable among these Telmex, the country's only telephone company, and a case study in high prices and inefficiency. In the late 1980s and early 1990s, the sale of state-owned assets and a global economic recovery marked a brief return to the growth rates of the 1950s and 1960s.

Toward his last years in office, Salinas joined his U.S. and Canadian counterparts, President George H. W. Bush and Prime Minister Brian Mulroney, in negotiating what he considered his crowning achievement: the North American Free Trade Agreement (NAFTA). Implemented on January 1, 1994, long after Bush and Mulroney had both been voted out of office, NAFTA bound Canada, the United States, and Mexico together in a trade pact that abolished tariff barriers and protectionist legislation. Salinas hoped that NAFTA would boost trade with the United States and Canada and bring more jobs to Mexico, in particular from the U.S. textile industry, the CEOs of which salivated at the idea of transferring jobs to a country where the minimum wage did not exceed $3 a day. Indeed, during its first decade of existence, NAFTA has provided an important stimulus to the U.S.-Mexican border region.

But NAFTA came at a steep price. The agreement necessitated significant revisions to the nationalist provisions of the Constitution of 1917, in particular the strictures imposed on foreign ownership of the subsoil. In a sense, Mexico had come full circle in embracing Porfirian laissez-faire policies regarding foreign investments. In fact, the old dictator would have winced at the idea that the Mexican government was no longer free to adopt any trade restrictions and award preferential treatment to investors of its choice. Many Mexicans resisted the idea of selling of their country's assets to the highest bidder. Of equal concern was the fact that NAFTA—unlike the successive treaties that had created the European Union (EU), the world's largest trading bloc—did not contain immigration provisions. While citizens of the EU countries could freely relocate across national boundaries, millions of Mexican immigrants in the United States and Canada remained undocumented and without legal status. Finally, the impact of NAFTA was uneven across Mexico: while the north boomed due to its close ties to the United States, the rural economies of the central and southern states continued to decline, a decline exacerbated by the elimination of important protections for campesinos in the constitution.

The most significant resistance movement against NAFTA occurred in the southeastern state of Chiapas, home to a new insurgent army, the Ejército Zapatista de Liberación Nacional (EZLN, or Zapatista Army of National Liberation). Named after the revolutionary leader Zapata, who lost his life fighting for land and liberty for Mexico's indigenous campesinos, the EZLN seized a wide swath of land in central Chiapas beginning on January 1, 1994, the day NAFTA took effect. Led by the enigmatic Rafael Guillén, or "Subcomandante Marcos," the Zapatistas demanded a radical effort to address the plight of the country's indigenous campesinos, and particularly the impoverished Maya of Chiapas. Marcos also announced demands for abrogation of NAFTA, or at least the negotiation of amendments that would prevent the sale of ejidos to private investors. The movement adopted new tactics, vowing nonviolence and distributing its message across the Internet. In response, the Salinas administration avoided the mistake of repeating Echeverría's violent crackdown in the 1970s. Still, Salinas refused to negotiate, and government forces waged a war of attrition on the EZLN, attempting to starve the movement by cutting off access to food. It was only through the actions of volunteers who sneaked food and other essentials past a ring of military forces that the EZLN could survive for years in rural Chiapas.

The Zapatista rebellion began a very bad year for the Salinas administration. No sooner had Mexicans digested the news of its appearance than another shocking development rocked the nation. In March 1994, a gunman assassinated Luis Donaldo Colosio, the presidential nominee and hence certain successor to Salinas. Prior to his assassination, Colosio had announced plans to democratize Mexico, end the dominance of the PRI, and reform the party. Many Mexicans immediately blamed the assassination on Salinas, whom they suspected of killing the man he had handpicked because Colosio had proven too independent for the president's liking. The truth about the assassination never came out. Even as Mexicans argued about the identity of the culprits of this crime and Salinas selected another nominee, his former finance minister, Luis Zedillo, a series of high-profile kidnappings of entrepreneurs scared domestic and foreign investors alike. As a result, investors sold peso-denominated assets, forcing the Salinas administration to sell more than $10 billion (or more than one-third) of the country's foreign-currency reserves to avoid devaluation of the national currency. Things got even worse for Salinas in September with the assassination of PRI Secretary General José Francisco Ruiz Massieu. Soon thereafter, rising U.S. interest rates induced more investors to sell their Mexican assets, producing a massive capital flight that caused a significant devaluation of the peso. As a result of its earlier decision to sell off currency reserves, the Salinas administration could do nothing to stop the peso's downslide. When the dust had cleared, the peso had lost two-thirds of its value against the dollar. If there was a silver lining in this debacle, it was that the damage was not nearly as severe as in 1982. The existence of NAFTA limited the peso's devaluation: concerned about the potential fallout from this crisis for the U.S. economy, the administration of U.S. President Bill Clinton rapidly assembled an aid package that prevented the peso from declining even further.

The peso crisis of 1994 engendered the growth of conservative grass-roots movements critical of the government's handling of the economy. Perhaps most important among these groups was El Barzón (in English, the horse-drawn plow), a movement of farmers and small-scale entrepreneurs who had acquired significant debts on a dollar basis. The peso's decline doubled the debtors' obligations to the banks in terms of the national currency, and the crisis also led to higher interest rates for new and adjustable loans. El Barzón members subscribed to the revolutionary-era slogan *"Debo, no niego, pago lo justo"* ("I owe, I do not deny it; I will pay what is fair"). Members of the group started random protests in Chihuahua and Sonora. In the central state of Zacatecas, El Barzón even organized partial road blocks as part of its protest, leading to the arrest of some of its ring leaders. The emergence of groups such as this one was bad news indeed for the PRI, which faced the desertion of much of its remaining support among the middle class.

The tale of Mercedes Pacheco, as told by the Canadian sociologist Judith Adler Hellman, illustrates the far greater struggles of the poor majority. Pacheco was an indigenous woman who had moved to Mexico City at the age of eight to escape the stark poverty in her village. At forty-three years of age, she sold mangos, apples, and candy at the Mercado Argentina, a public market a few blocks from the Zócalo. Her place in the market was dependent on her good relations with a female political boss and PRI candidate for Congress, who received kickbacks from Pacheco in return for guaranteeing her space in the market. Working a seven-day week, Mercedes earned between $60 and $80 U.S. a month before the peso devaluation. The NAFTA agreement meant little to her; as she told Hellman just before giving her a bag of mangos too overripe to sell, it "is for rich people. It's not meant to help people like me."

As a president who had only come to power as a replacement of a highly popular candidate, Zedillo, who replaced Salinas, realized that the PRI had finally reached the twilight of its undisputed rule. Already in 1988, Salinas had won a highly questionable victory over the left-wing opposition candidate Cuauhtémoc Cárdenas amidst allegations of fraud. Since that time, the PRI had steadily lost influence in northern and central Mexico to the conservative PAN. Zedillo understood well that his own legacy could either consist in prolonging the rule of the PRI by illegal means or by serving as the president who at long last brought democracy to Mexico. As a result, he consented to a wide-ranging electoral reform that gave greater opportunities to opposition parties at the precise moment when the PAN offered a charismatic leader, the former rancher and Coca-Cola executive, Vicente Fox Quesada. On July 2, 2000, voters went to the polls and ousted the PRI after seventy-one years, with Fox receiving 42 percent of the vote, 7 percent more than PRI candidate Francisco Labastida. Although the PRI remained the largest party in Congress, it had lost hold of Los Pinos, the presidential residence. Democracy had finally arrived in Mexico, and the revolution had officially ended with the demise of the PRI.

Mexicans had high expectations of Fox, believing that he would curb corruption and provide accountable, transparent government. After the U.S. Supreme Court declared Republican George W. Bush the winner of the 2000 presidential elections, supporters from PAN also hoped that Fox's conservative and probusiness credentials would allow him to develop a close relationship with the U.S. executive. Indeed, Bush announced his intention to work closely with Fox, and in particular to negotiate a new immigration agreement. For his part, Fox declared that he would abandon Mexico's time-tested nationalist foreign policy in favor of collaborating with the United States in the democratization of the world.

Ultimately, however, the new government could not fulfill the high expectations that Mexicans had placed on it, and those who had believed that Fox's triumph signaled the beginning of a new era were to be sorely disappointed. Many Mexicans who supported Fox demanded change, but few asked how the new leader would effect change. Faced with such high expectations, Fox was destined to disappoint. Contrary to the expectations of strict Catholics within PAN, the new president did not move to outlaw abortion, and against the wishes of the powerful business sector, he also made no effort to privatize PEMEX. When it came to the issue of corruption, Fox also appeared to be more similar to his predecessors than his supporters had believed. Just weeks after his inauguration on December 1, 2000, word leaked out that the president had ordered a number of extraordinarily expensive towels for his own use in Los Pinos. In his defense, however, Fox faced impossible odds in bringing about rapid change in a system that had been dominated by one party for 71 years. The president did not have a majority in a Congress divided among three parties, and the 2003 elections ushered in a legislature once again dominated by the PRI. Under those circumstances, progress was painfully slow. Even worse, regional unrest—and most recently, a bloody standoff in Oaxaca between a PRI governor and the Asamblea Popular de los Pueblos de Oaxaca (APPO, or Popular Assembly of the Peoples of Oaxaca)—plagued the Fox administration.

Economic issues compounded Fox's difficulties. Although NAFTA had shifted some jobs south of the border during the 1990s, China's entry into the World Trade Organization in 2001 reversed this trend. This step eliminated trade barriers with the world's most populous country, a nation that was to experience one of the highest economic growth rates during the next five years. Mexico's manufacturing base could not compete with that of China, India, and other emerging industrial nations in Asia, and by the end of the Fox administration competition with these nations had undone the gains that Mexican manufacturing had made through NAFTA. To this day, the country's manufacturing sector continues to struggle, and raw material exports and remittances from Mexicans living abroad make up the two most significant sources of foreign-source income.

Finally, his strong alliance with President George W. Bush became an albatross around the neck of Fox. The new immigration deal vanished in the aftermath of the terrorist attacks of September 11, 2001, as both Bush and the U.S. Congress emphasized national security issues over bilateral U.S.-Mexican concerns. Hoping that Bush would reward staunch allies down the road, Fox supported the United States in the post-9/11 fallout. But soon thereafter, Fox and his fellow Mexicans witnessed the ill effects of beefed-up security measures along the U.S.-Mexico border. The U.S. invasion of Iraq in March 2003 was another problem for Mexico, as this sort of "pre-emptive" strike against a sovereign nation violated the most basic precepts of Mexican foreign policy. Anxious to avoid a standoff with the United States over this issue, Fox suffered the misfortune of Mexico's being a member of the Security Council of the United Nations during the months leading up to the invasion. Thus the Mexican representative in the Security Council faced votes on aggressively worded resolutions against Iraqi leader Saddam Hussein—resolutions introduced by Bush in order to procure international sanction for his war plans. Until the invasion, Fox consistently advocated dialogue and negotiation and demanded proof of the Bush administration's charge that the Saddam Hussein regime was in possession of weapons of mass destruction. Coupled with his disappointment over the failure to negotiate an immigration agreement, the U.S. stand on Iraq damaged Fox's formerly excellent relations with Bush. But it also highlighted the fact that Fox had initially placed much of his political capital in an alliance that had not benefited Mexico. During Fox's last year in office, the Republican-led majority in the U.S. House of Representatives approved a strongly worded plan to reduce Mexican immigration to the United States, and even to criminalize undocumented entry into the country as a felony offense. Although the Senate failed to go along with the House plan, an immigration agreement appeared elusive at the time Fox left office in November 2006. In fact, Bush ordered the construction of 700 more miles of "fence" along the Mexico–United States border—a signal that the American president was more interested in law enforcement that in legalizing the status of millions of Mexicans who had resided and worked in the United States for many years.

Yet there was change during the Fox regime, in a realm in which most Mexicans least expected it. A year into his presidency, Fox married his former spokeswoman, Marta Sahagún, an outspoken woman who did not fit the mold of the meek, motherly first lady that the citizens had come to expect from the wife of their chief executive. Sahagún not only freely expressed her views on many subjects, but she also openly entertained thoughts of succeeding her husband in the presidency. Many of the conservative PAN supporters who had placed their hopes in Fox expressed dismay at a politically active first lady, let alone the specter of a female president.

The hotly contested presidential elections of 2006 were an important test for Mexico's newly democratic institutions. As we have seen at the beginning of this book, PRD candidate Andrés Manuel López Obrador, the former mayor of Mexico City, headed into the summer as the favorite, with both PRI candidate Roberto Madrazo and PAN candidate Felipe Calderón trailing him by double digits. In many ways, a victory for the PRD would have fully vindicated the electoral process as one that could produce a triumph for a candidate from each of the major parties. López Obrador also represented a neopopulist leadership style critical of neoliberal globalization that had swept candidates to the presidency of Bolivia, Brazil, and Chile, not to mention the authoritarian Hugo Chávez of Venezuela. Yet Mexico ended up bucking the regional trend, and the election showed the continued regional, political, and social divisions within the country. The nasty campaign, which ended with the major candidates hurling insults at each other, turned many Mexicans off from the political process. The close race ended up making voters even more suspicious, especially when the national elections board, the Instituto Federal Electoral (IFE), refused to name a winner on election night. The controversy about the election continued well into the fall, with López Obrador's supporters blocking the Paseo de la Reforma and other thoroughfares in Mexico City for weeks in protest against what they believed was a massive fraud committed against their candidate. On December 1, 2006, the conservative PAN candidate Calderón took the oath of office in front of Congress despite brawls between representatives from the PRD and PAN just hours before. Meanwhile, López Obrador led a demonstration at the Zócalo with more than 100,000 people in attendance.

As this volume goes to press, it is too early to judge the Calderón administration, currently in its first year in office. Its earliest test has consisted of dealing with its political opposition not only at the national level, but also at the state level, where conflicts persist in Chiapas, Oaxaca, and other states. Calderón has also vowed to confront organized crime in Mexico, particularly to cooperate with the United States in cracking down on his country's numerous drug lords. Democracy has made great strides in Mexico.

•••

Calderón's struggles to gain political legitimacy and other recent events highlight the persistence of the intricate Mexican mosaic that continues to baffle observers with its enduring complexity even amidst the homogenizing forces of globalization. In fact, the uneven impact of globalization on Mexico and its people has brought the country's cultural, social, and regional differences into stark focus, reminding observers that the Mexican mosaic is here to stay.

Many Mexicans—and particularly their national leaders—have long dreamed of a strong, unified country bound together by a clear sense of national identity. They have designed strategies to erase economic underdevelopment, to build a strong national state, and to forge a national culture in which all of Mexico's diverse people participate. Sometimes, these strategies have involved efforts to adopt foreign influences and make Mexico more like Western nations such as the United States, France, or Great Britain. This tendency was apparent first in the Bourbon Reforms of the late 1700s, in the era of Liberal modernization in the second half of the nineteenth century, and (to the greatest extent) in the contemporary era. At other junctures, Mexican leaders have sought to shield their country from negative global influences; for example, during the long era following the Mexican Revolution that only ended with the massive debt crisis of 1982. None of these attempts succeeded entirely, nor were any of them complete failures. At the beginning of the twenty-first century, Mexicans have reason to be proud of their nation's rich cultural and historical heritage, their diversified economy, and their new democratic structures. Yet underdevelopment, poverty, and elite rule continue to characterize much of Mexico, and tens of millions of Mexicans—like the street peddler whom readers encountered at the beginning of this book—still wait for the day when they fully participate in realizing the potential of this fascinating and complex nation.

❧ Bibliographical Essay ❧

*T*he literature on Mexican history is vast. The following pages only list some of the most important English-language works, including both primary sources and historical literature. The bibliographies and references in these works can serve as points of departure for finding additional resources.

Useful general histories include John Sherman, Michael C. Meyer, and Susan Deeds, *The Course of Mexican History*, 8th ed. (New York: Oxford University Press, 2007); Alicia Hernández Chávez, *Mexico: A Brief History*, trans. Andy Klatt (Berkeley: University of California Press, 2006); Colin MacLachlan and William H. Beezley, *El Gran Pueblo: A History of Greater Mexico*, 3rd ed. (Upper Saddle River, NJ: Prentice Hall, 2003); Michael C. Meyer and William H. Beezley, eds., *The Oxford History of Mexico* (Oxford: Oxford University Press, 2000); Douglas W. Richmond, *The Mexican Nation: Historical Continuity and Modern Change* (Upper Saddle River, NJ: Prentice Hall, 2001); and Leslie Bethell, ed., *Mexico Since Independence* (Cambridge: Cambridge University Press, 1991). Interesting vignettes of individual Mexicans during the period since c. 1750 can be found in Jeffrey Pilcher, ed., *The Human Tradition in Mexico* (Wilmington, DE: SR Books, 2004).

For collections of primary sources on the history of Mexico, consult Gilbert M. Joseph and Timothy J. Henderson, *The Mexico Reader: History, Culture, Politics* (Durham, NC: Duke University Press, 2002), W. Dirk Raat, ed., *Mexico from Independence to Revolution, 1810–1910* (Lincoln: University of Nebraska Press, 1982); W. Dirk Raat and William H. Beezley, eds., *Twentieth-Century Mexico* (Lincoln: University of Nebraska Press, 1986); and Jürgen Buchenau, ed. and trans., *Mexico OtherWise: Modern Mexico in the Eyes of Foreign Observers* (Albuquerque: University of New Mexico Press, 2005).

131

Chapter One

There is an abundant literature on preconquest Mexico. On the beginnings of indigenous civilizations, see Richard E. W. Adams, *Prehistoric Mesoamerica*, 3rd ed., (Norman: University of Oklahoma Press, 2005). For studies of the Maya and Toltecs, consult Linda Schele and David Friedel, *A Forest of Kings: The Untold Story of the Ancient Maya* (New York: William Morrow & Co., 1990); Michael D. Coe, *From the Olmecs to the Aztecs* (London: Thames and Hudson, 1994); and Enrique Florescano, *The Myth of Quetzalcóatl*, trans. Lisa Hochroth (Baltimore: Johns Hopkins University Press, 1999). The Aztec Empire is the subject of Inga Clendinnen, *Aztecs: An Interpretation* (New York: Cambridge University Press, 1991; Frances F. Berdan et al., *Aztec Imperial Strategies* (Washington, DC: Dumbarton Oaks, 1993); and Ross Hassig, *Aztec Warfare: Imperial Expansion and Political Control* (Norman: University of Oklahoma Press, 1988), among others. On city size in post-Classic Mesoamerica, see Michael E. Smith, "City Size in Late Post-Classic Mesoamerica," *Journal of Urban History* 31.4 (May 2005): 403–34.

The Spanish conquest has generated an impressive scholarship. For some of the most significant recent works, see Ross Hassig, *Mexico and the Spanish Conquest*, 2nd ed. (Norman: University of Oklahoma Press, 2006); Matthew Restall, *Seven Myths of the Spanish Conquest* (Oxford: Oxford University Press, 2003); Camilla Townsend, *Malintzín's Choices: An Indian Woman in the Conquest of Mexico* (Albuquerque: University of New Mexico Press, 2006); Stuart Schwartz, *Victors and Vanquished: Spanish and Nahua Views of the Conquest of Mexico* (New York: Bedford/St. Martin's, 2000); and Grant D. Jones, *The Conquest of the Last Maya Kingdom* (Stanford, CA: Stanford University Press, 1998). An older and still influential work is Robert C. Padden, *The Hummingbird and the Hawk: Conquest and Sovereignty in the Valley of Mexico, 1503–1541* (New York: Harper and Row, 1970).

Primary sources on the conquest of Mexico include the conquistadors' version of events as well as editions of Aztec documents and oral histories. The most important chronicles by the conquistadors are Hernán Cortés, *Letters from Mexico*, ed. and trans. Anthony Padgen (New Haven, CT: Yale University Press, 2001); Bernal Díaz del Castillo, *The Conquest of New Spain*, trans. John M. Cohen (London: Penguin, 1963); and Francisco López de Gómara, *Cortés: The Life of the Conqueror of Mexico by His Secretary, Francisco López de Gómara*, ed. and trans. Lesley Byrd Simpson (Berkeley: University of California Press, 1966). For an Aztec vision of the conquest as compiled by a Mexican anthropologist, see Miguel León-Portilla, ed., *The Broken Spears: The Aztec Account of the Conquest of*

Mexico (Boston: Beacon Press, 1992). Written by Spanish clergy in New Spain, other significant first-hand accounts influenced by indigenous perspectives are Bernardino de Sahagún, *Florentine Codex: General History of the Things of New Spain* (Santa Fe, NM: School of American Research, 1950–1982); Alonso de Zorita, *Life and Labor in Ancient Mexico: The Brief and Summary Relation of the Lords of New Spain*, trans. Benjamin Keen (Norman: University of Oklahoma Press, 1994); and Diego de Landa, *Yucatán Before and After the Conquest*, trans. William Gates (Dover Publications, 1937). On the aftermath of the conquest, and particularly the exploitation of native peoples through the encomienda, see Bartolomé de las Casas, *The Devastation of the Indies: A Brief Account*, trans. Herma Briffault (Baltimore, MD: Johns Hopkins University Press, 1992).

There is also a vast literature on the transformation of colonial society by miscegenation, indigenous population decline, and the importation of African slaves. On population decline, consult Alfred W. Crosby, *The Columbian Exchange: Ecological and Cultural Consequences of 1492* (Westport, CT: Greenwood Press, 1972). For the history of the indigenous population of Mexico after the conquest, see James Lockhart, *The Nahuas After the Conquest: A Social and Cultural History of the Indians of Central Mexico, Sixteenth Through Eighteenth Centuries* (Stanford, CA: Stanford University Press, 1994); Charles Gibson, *The Aztecs under Spanish Rule: A History of the Indians of the Valley of Mexico, 1519–1810* (Stanford, CA: Stanford University Press, 1964); Inga Clendinnen, *Ambivalent Conquests: Maya and Spaniard in Yucatán, 1517–1570* (Cambridge: Cambridge University Press, 1987), and Nancy M. Farriss, *Maya Society under Colonial Rule: The Collective Enterprise of Survival* (Princeton, NJ: Princeton University Press, 1984). Regarding Africans in colonial Mexico, see Ben Vinson III., *Bearing Arms for His Majesty: The Free-Colored Militia in Colonial Mexico* (Stanford, CA: Stanford University Press, 2004); Herman L. Bennett, *Africans In Colonial Mexico: Absolutism, Christianity, and Afro-Creole Consciousness, 1570–1640* (Bloomington: Indiana University Press, 2003); and Colin Palmer, *Slaves of the White God: Blacks in Mexico, 1570–1650* (Cambridge, MA: Harvard University Press, 1976).

Another significant body of literature deals with colonial administration, economy and commerce. On administration, see Mark A. Burkholder, "An Empire Beyond Compare," in *The Oxford History of Mexico*, eds. Michael C. Meyer and William H. Beezley, 115–49 (Oxford: Oxford University Press, 2000); Woodrow Borah, *Justice By Insurance: The General Indian Court and the Legal Aides of the Half-Real* (Berkeley: University of California Press, 1983); Robert Haskett, *Indigenous Rulers: An Ethnohistory of Town Government in Colonial Cuernavaca* (Albuquerque: University of New Mexico Press, 1991). The frontier is the subject of David J. Weber, *The Spanish Frontier in North America* (New

Haven, CT: Yale University Press, 1992). Regarding the colonial economy and trade, see Louisa S. Hoberman, *Mexico's Merchant Elite, 1590–1660: Silver, State, and Society* (Durham, NC: Duke University Press, 1991); John E. Kicza, *Colonial Entrepreneurs: Families and Business in Bourbon Mexico City* (Albuquerque: University of New Mexico Press, 1983); Edith B. Couturier, *The Silver King: The Remarkable Life of the Count of Regla in Colonial Mexico* (Albuquerque: University of New Mexico Press, 2003); and David A. Brading, *Miners and Merchants in Bourbon Mexico* (Cambridge: Cambridge University Press, 1971). Studies of the colonial hacienda include Eric Van Young, *Hacienda and Market in Eighteenth-Century Mexico: The Rural Economy of the Guadalajara Region, 1675–1820* (Berkeley: University of California Press, 1981): For a first-hand description of the late colonial economy and politics, see Alexander von Humboldt, *Political Essay on the Kingdom of New Spain*, trans. John Black [1811], ed. Mary Maples Dunn (New York: Alfred Knopf, 1972).

Yet another important area of scholarship is the colonial church. See William B. Taylor, *Magistrates of the Sacred: Priests and Parishioners in Eighteenth-Century Mexico* (Stanford, CA: Stanford University Press, 1996); Pamela Voekel, *Alone Before God: The Religious Origins of Modernity in Mexico* (Durham, NC: Duke University Press, 2002); John F. Schwaller, *The Church and Clergy in Sixteenth-Century Mexico* (Albuquerque: University of New Mexico Press, 1987); and Richard E. Greenleaf, *The Mexican Inquisition of the Sixteenth Century* (Albuquerque: University of New Mexico Press, 1969). For the cult of Guadalupe, see Stafford Poole, *Our Lady of Guadalupe: The Origins and Sources of a Mexican National Symbol, 1531–1797* (Tucson: University of Arizona Press, 1995). Catalina de Erauso tells her story in Catalina de Erauso, *Lieutenant Nun: Transvestite in the New World*, eds. Michele Stepto and Gabriel Stepto (Boston: Beacon Press, 1997). Another important study that demonstrates the fluidity of identity despite ostensibly rigid religious norms is Richard Boyer, *Lives of the Bigamists: Marriage, Family, and Community in Colonial Mexico* (Albuquerque: University of New Mexico Press, 1985).

Regarding gender in colonial Mexico, consult Susan M. Socolow, *The Women of Colonial Latin America* (New York: Cambridge University Press, 2000); Patricia Seed, *To Love, Honor, and Obey in Colonial Mexico: Conflicts over Marriage Choice, 1574–1821* (Stanford, CA: Stanford University Press, 1988); Susan Schroeder et al., eds., *Indian Women of Early Mexico* (Norman: University of Oklahoma Press, 1997); and Asunción Lavrín, "Women in Colonial Mexico," in *The Oxford History of Mexico*, eds. Michael C. Meyer and William H. Beezley, 245–73 (Oxford: Oxford University Press, 2000).

Even before the coming of the independence movement, Spanish authority over its colonies remained contested. On riots and rebellions, consult Andrew L. Knaut, *The Pueblo Revolt of 1680: Conquest and Resistance in Seventeenth-Century New Mexico* (Norman: University of Oklahoma Press, 1995); William B. Taylor, *Drinking, Homicide, and Rebellion in Colonial Mexican Villages* (Stanford, CA: Stanford University Press, 1979); R. Douglas Cope, *The Limits of Racial Domination: Plebeian Society in Colonial Mexico City, 1660–1720* (Madison: University of Wisconsin Press, 1994); Susan Schroeder, *Native Resistance and the Pax Colonial in New Spain* (Lincoln: University of Nebraska Press, 1998); and J. I. Israel, *Race, Class, and Politics in Colonial Mexico, 1610–1670* (Oxford: Oxford University Press, 1975). The emergence of Mexican national identity among the colonial elite is the subject of Jacques Lafaye, *Quetzalcóatl and Guadalupe: The Formation of Mexican National Consciousness, 1531–1813*, trans. Benjamin Keen (Chicago: University of Chicago Press, 1976); and David Brading, *The First America: The Spanish Monarchy, Creole Patriots, and the Liberal State, 1492–1866* (Cambridge: Cambridge University Press, 1992).

CHAPTER TWO

Good studies of the independence period include Eric Van Young, *The Other Rebellion: Popular Violence, Ideology, and the Mexican Struggle for Independence* (Stanford, CA: Stanford University Press, 2001); John Tutino, *From Insurrection to Revolution in Mexico: Social Bases of Agrarian Violence, 1750–1940* (Princeton, NJ: Princeton University Press, 1986); Christon Archer, *The Birth of Modern Mexico, 1780–1824* (Wilmington, DE: SR Books, 2003); Jaime E. Rodríguez O., ed., *The Independence of Mexico and the Creation of the New Nation* (Los Angeles: University of California, Los Angeles, Latin American Center, 1989); Hugh Hamill, *The Hidalgo Revolt: Prelude to Mexican Independence* (Gainesville: University of Florida Press, 1966); and Romeo Flores Caballero, *Counterrevolution: The Role of the Spaniards in the Independence of Mexico* (Lincoln: University of Nebraska Press, 1974).

For the early national period, good starting points are Timothy E. Anna, *Forging Mexico, 1821–1835* (Lincoln: University of Nebraska Press, 2001); *Ibid., The Mexican Empire of Iturbide* (Lincoln: University of Nebraska Press, 1990); and Will Fowler, *Mexico in the Age of Proposals, 1821–1853* (Westport, CT: Greenwood Press, 1998). The Liberal-Conservative debate is analyzed in Charles A. Hale, *Mexican Liberalism in the Age of Mora* (New Haven, CT: Yale University Press, 1968). On Santa Anna, see Will Fowler, *Santa Anna of Mexico*

(Lincoln: University of Nebraska Press, 2007); and Shannon Baker, "Santa Anna's Search for Personalized Nationalism," in *Heroes and Hero Cults in Latin America*, eds. Samuel Brunk and Ben Fallaw, 58–82 (Austin: University of Texas Press, 2006). For travel accounts offering different perspectives of this period, see Joel R. Poinsett, *Notes on Mexico Made in the Autumn of 1822, Accompanied by an Historical Sketch of the Revolution* (New York: Praeger, 1969); Fanny Calderón de la Barca, *Life in Mexico during a Residence of Two Years in that Country* (London: Chapman and Hall, 1843); and Carl C. Sartorius, *Mexico: Landscape and Popular Sketches* (Darmstadt, London, and New York, 1858).

On the numerous foreign interventions in Mexico during the nineteenth century, see Harold D. Sims, *The Expulsion of Mexico's Spaniards, 1821–1936* (Pittsburgh: University of Pittsburgh Press, 1990); and Nettie Lee Benson, "Territorial Integrity in Mexican Politics, 1821–1833," in *The Independence of Mexico and the Creation of the New Nation*, ed. Jaime E. Rodríguez O. (Los Angeles: University of California, Los Angeles, Latin American Center, 1989). The literature on the Texas secession includes Andrés Tijerino, *Tejanos in Texas under the Mexican Flag, 1821–1836* (College Station: Texas A&M University Press, 1994). Regarding the U.S.–Mexican War, see Timothy J. Henderson, *A Glorious Defeat: Mexico and Its War with the United States* (New York: Hill and Wang, 2007); Richard V. Francaviglia and Douglas W. Richmond, eds., *Dueling Eagles: Reinterpreting the U.S.–Mexican War, 1846–1848* (Ft. Worth: Texas Christian University Press, 2000); and Pedro Santoni, *Mexicans at Arms: Puro Federalists and the Politics of War, 1846–1848* (Ft. Worth: Texas Christian University Press, 1996). For the perspective of U.S. soldiers in Mexico, see William S. Henry, *Campaign Sketches of the War with Mexico* (New York: Harper and Brothers, 1847); and George W. Kendall, *Dispatches from the Mexican War* (Norman: University of Oklahoma Press, 1999).

The literature on the Reforma era includes Richard N. Sinkin, *Mexican Reform, 1855–1876* (Austin: University of Texas Press, 1980); Florencia E. Mallon, *Peasant and Nation: The Making of Postcolonial Mexico and Peru* (Berkeley: University of California Press, 1995); David Thomson and Guy P.C. LaFrance, *Patriotism, Politics, and Popular Liberalism in Nineteenth-Century Mexico: Juan Francisco Lucas and the Puebla Sierra* (Wilmington, DE: SR Books, 2002); and Charles R. Berry, *The Reform in Oaxaca, 1856–1876: A Microhistory of the Liberal Revolution* (Lincoln: University of Nebraska Press, 1981). A good biography of Benito Juárez is Brian Hamnett, *Juárez* (London: Longman, 1994). For Juárez's legacy, see Charles Weeks, *The Juárez Myth in Mexico* (Tuscaloosa: University of Alabama Press, 1987). Regarding the role of the United States, see Donathon C. Olliff, *Reforma Mexico and the United States: The Search for Alternatives to Annexation*

(Tuscaloosa: University of Alabama Press, 1981); and Thomas D. Schoonover, *Dollars Over Dominion: The Triumph of Liberalism in Mexican-United States Relations* (Baton Rouge: Louisiana State University Press, 1978).

On the French Intervention and Emperor Maximilian, see Bertita Harding, *Phantom Crown: The Story of Maximilian and Carlota of Mexico* (Mexico City: Ediciones Tolteca, 1960); and Erika Pani, "Dreaming of a Mexican Empire: The Political Projects of the 'Imperialistas,'" *Hispanic American Historical Review* 82.1 (2002): 1–31. For first-person accounts by members of Maximilian's and Carlota's court, consult Paula von Kollonitz, *The Court of Mexico*, 2nd ed., trans. J. E. Ollivant (London: Saunders, Otley, and Co., 1868); and Samuel M. Basch, *Recollections of Mexico: The Last Ten Months of Maximilian's Empire* (Wilmington, DE: SR Books, 2001).

A good survey of the social and cultural history of nineteenth-century Mexico is Mark Wasserman, *Everyday Life and Politics in Nineteenth-Century Mexico: Men, Women, and War* (Albuquerque: University of New Mexico Press, 2000). More specific studies include Silvia M. Arrom, *Containing the Poor: The Mexico City Poor House, 1774–1871* (Durham, NC: Duke University Press, 2000); Marie E. Francois, *A Culture of Everyday Credit: Housekeeping, Pawnbroking, and Governance in Mexico City, 1750–1920* (Lincoln: University of Nebraska Press, 2007); Peter Guardino, *Peasants, Politics, and the Formation of Mexico's National State: Guerrero, 1800–1857* (Stanford, CA: Stanford University Press, 2002); Michael T. Ducey, *A Nation of Villages: Riot and Rebellion in the Mexican Huasteca, 1750–1850* (Tucson: University of Arizona Press, 2004); and Margaret Chowning, *Wealth and Power in Provincial Mexico: Michoacán from the Late Colony to the Revolution* (Stanford, CA: Stanford University Press, 1999). For the caste war of Yucatán, see Don E. Dumond, *The Machete and the Cross: Campesino Rebellion in Yucatán* (Lincoln: University of Nebraska Press, 1997); and Nelson Reed, *The Caste War of Yucatán* (Stanford, CA: Stanford University Press, 1964). Yaqui resistance in Sonora is the subject of Evelyn Hu-Dehart, *Yaqui Resistance and Survival: The Struggle for Land and Autonomy, 1821–1910* (Madison: University of Wisconsin Press, 1984).

CHAPTER THREE

There are many good studies on the modernization project, including John Coatsworth, *Growth Against Development: The Economic Impact of Railroads in Porfirian Mexico* (DeKalb: Northern Illinois University Press, 1981); and Robert H. Holden, *Mexico and the Survey of Public Lands, 1876–1911: The Management of Modernization* (DeKalb: Northern Illinois University Press, 1994). On rurales and banditry, see Paul Vanderwood, *Disorder and Progress: Bandits, Police, and Mexican Development*, 2nd ed. (Wilmington, DE: SR Books, 1992). Laurens B. Perry, *Juárez and Díaz: Machine Politics in Mexico* (DeKalb: Northern Illinois University Press, 1979), makes a compelling case for viewing both Juárez and Díaz in a continuum of political and economic modernization. Don M. Coerver, *The Porfirian Interregnum: The Presidency of Manuel González of Mexico, 1880–1884* (Fort Worth: Texas Christian University Press, 1979), analyzes the critical early 1880s and the establishment of the Porfirian system. Immigration and the emergence of consumer culture is the subject of the first two chapters of Jürgen Buchenau, *Tools of Progress: A German Merchant Family in Mexico City, 1865–Present* (Albuquerque: University of New Mexico Press, 2004). A regional comparison can be found in Thomas Benjamin and William McNellie, *Other Mexicos: Essays on Regional Mexican History, 1876–1910* (Albuquerque: University of New Mexico Press, 1984). A good general biography of Díaz is Paul Garner, *Porfirio Díaz* (London: Longman, 2001). The Tomochic episode in the introduction to the chapter is compellingly analyzed in Paul Vanderwood, *The Power of God Against the Guns of Government: Religious Upheaval in Mexico at the Turn of the Nineteenth Century* (Stanford, CA: Stanford University Press, 1998). Regarding industrialization, see Stephen Haber, *Industry and Underdevelopment: The Industrialization of Mexico, 1880–1940* (Stanford, CA: Stanford University Press, 1989); and Alex M. Saragoza, *The Monterrey Elite and the Mexican State* (Austin: University of Texas Press, 1988).

On Porfirian society and culture, see William Beezley, *Judas at the Jockey Club and Other Episodes of Porfirian Mexico* (Lincoln: University of Nebraska Press, 1987); William E. French, *A Peaceful and Working People: Manners, Morals, and Class Formation in Northern Mexico* (Albuquerque: University of New Mexico Press, 1996); Pablo Piccato, *City of Suspects: Crime in Mexico City, 1900–1931* (Durham: Duke University Press, 2001); and Michael Johns, *The City of Mexico in the Age of Díaz* (Austin: University of Texas Press, 1997). On the científicos and Mexican positivist thought, see Charles Hale, *The Transformation of Liberalism in Late Nineteenth-Century Mexico* (Princeton, NJ: Princeton University Press, 1989), and W. Dirk Raat, "Ideas and Society in Don Porfirio's Mexico," *The Americas* 30.1 (July 1973): 32–53. On education, see Mary Kay Vaughan, *The State, Education, and Social Class in Mexico, 1880–1928* (DeKalb: Northern Illinois University Press, 1982). For foreign relations and the international image of Mexico in the Porfirian era, see Mauricio Tenorio Trillo, *Mexico at the World's Fairs: Crafting a Modern Nation* (Berkeley: University of California Press, 1996), and Jürgen Buchenau, *In the Shadow of the Giant: The Making of Mexico's Central America Policy, 1876–1930* (Tuscaloosa: University of Alabama Press, 1996).

The Porfirian era gave rise to an extensive travel literature. For conditions at the beginning of the Porfiriato, see Fanny Chambers Gooch [Iglehart], *Face to Face with the Mexicans: The Domestic Life, Educational, Social, and Business Ways, Statesmanship and Literature, Legendary and General History of the Mexican People as Seen and Studied by an American Woman During Seven Years of Intercourse with Them* (New York: Fords, Howard, and Hulbert, 1887); and Solomon B. Griffin, *Mexico of To-Day* (New York: Harper and Brothers, 1886). For a positive assessment, see Charles M. Flandrau, *Viva Mexico!* (New York: D. Appleton & Co., 1908). On the indigenous population, consult Carl Lumholtz, *Unknown Mexico: A Record of Five Years' Exploration Among the Tribes of the Western Sierra Madre; in the Tierra Caliente of Tepic and Jalisco; and Among the Tarascos of Michoacán* (London: MacMillan and Co., 1903). The most scathing critique of the last years of the Porfiriato is John Kenneth Turner, *Barbarous Mexico* (New York: Cassell, 1912).

For the crisis of the Porfiriato, consult James D. Cockcroft, *Intellectual Precursors of the Mexican Revolution, 1900–1913* (Austin: University of Texas Press, 1968); Jonathan C. Brown, "Foreign and Native-Born Workers in Porfirian Mexico," *American Historical Review* 98 (1993): 786–818; W. Dirk Raat, "The Diplomacy of Suppression: Los Revoltosos, Mexico, and the United States, 1906–1911," *Hispanic American Historical Review* 56 (1976): 529–60; Ramón Ruiz, *The People of Sonora and the Yankee Capitalists* (Tucson: University of Arizona Press, 1988); and William K. Meyers, *Forge of Progress, Crucible of Revolt: The Origins of the Mexican Revolution in the Comarca Lagunera, 1880–1911* (Albuquerque: University of New Mexico Press, 1994).

CHAPTER FOUR

The literature on the Mexican Revolution is among the most extensive on any subject of Latin American history. Useful syntheses are Alan Knight, *The Mexican Revolution*, 2 vols. (Cambridge: Cambridge University Press, 1986); John M. Hart, *Revolutionary Mexico: The Coming and Process of the Mexican Revolution* (Berkeley: University of California Press, 1987); Michael Gonzales, *The Mexican Revolution, 1910–1940* (Albuquerque: University of New Mexico Press, 2002); Adolfo Gilly, *The Mexican Revolution: A People's History* (New York: New Press, 2006); and Héctor Aguilar Camín and Lorenzo Meyer, *In the Shadow of the Mexican Revolution: Contemporary Mexican History, 1910–1989*, trans. Luis Alberto Fierro (Austin: University of Texas Press, 1993). On the role of the United States and other foreign powers, see Friedrich Katz, *The Secret War in Mexico: Europe, the United States, and the Mexican Revolution* (Chicago: University of Chicago Press, 1981); and Mark T. Gilderhus, *Diplomacy and Revolution: U.S.-Mexican Relations under Wilson and Carranza* (Tucson: The University of Arizona Press, 1977). On the myth of the revolution and how it evolved over time, see Thomas Benjamin, *La Revolución: Mexico's Great Revolution as Memory, Myth, and History* (Austin: University of Texas Press, 2000), and Ilene V. O'Malley, *The Myth of the Revolution: Hero Cults and the Institutionalization of the Mexican State, 1920–1940* (New York: Greenwood Press, 1979).

On the principal protagonists of the first decade of the revolution, see John Womack, *Emiliano Zapata and the Mexican Revolution* (New York: Knopf, 1968); Samuel Brunk, *Emiliano Zapata: Revolution and Betrayal in Mexico* (Albuquerque: University of New Mexico Press, 1995); William H. Beezley, "Madero, the 'Unknown' President and His Political Failure to Organize Rural Mexico," in *Essays on the Mexican Revolution: Revisionist Views of the Leaders*, eds. George Wolfskill and Douglas W. Richmond (Austin: University of Texas Press, 1979), 1–24; Peter V. N. Henderson, *In the Absence of Don Porfirio: Francisco León de la Barra and the Mexican Revolution* (Wilmington, DE: SR Books, 2000); Michael C. Meyer, *Huerta: A Political Portrait* (Lincoln: University of Nebraska Press, 1972); Friedrich Katz, *The Life and Times of Pancho Villa* (Stanford, CA: Stanford University Press, 1998); Douglas W. Richmond, *Venustiano Carranza's Nationalist Struggle, 1893–1920* (Lincoln: University of Nebraska Press, 1983); and Linda B. Hall, *Alvaro Obregón: Power and Revolution in Mexico, 1911–1920* (College Station: Texas A&M University Press, 1981).

There are numerous primary sources on the Mexican Revolution available in English, including travel accounts such as Rosa E. King, *Tempest over Mexico* (Boston: Little, Brown, and Co., 1935); John S. Reed, *Insurgent Mexico* (New York: D. Appleton & Co., 1914); Carleton Beals, *Mexican Maze* (Philadelphia: Lippincott, 1931); Graham Greene, *The Lawless Roads*, 3rd ed. (London: Heineman, 1950); Evelyn Waugh, *Mexico: An Object Lesson* (Boston: Little, Brown, and Co., 1939); and Verna C. Millán, *Mexico Reborn* (Boston: Houghton Mifflin, 1939), among many others. A great pictorial record is Anita Brenner and George R. Leighton, *The Wind that Swept Mexico* (New York: Harper, 1943).

There is also a vast and growing literature on social and cultural history. On gender, see Elizabeth Salas, *Soldaderas in the Mexican Military: Myth and History* (Austin: University of Texas Press, 1990); Katherine E. Bliss, *Compromised Positions: Prostitution, Public Health, and Gender Politics in Revolutionary Mexico City* (University Park: Penn State University Press, 2001); Jocelyn Olcott, *Revolutionary Women in Post-Revolutionary Mexico* (Durham, NC: Duke University Press, 2006); and Jocelyn Olcott, Mary Kay Vaughan, and Gabriela Cano, eds., *Sex in Revolution: Gender, Politics, and Power in Modern Mexico* (Durham, NC: Duke University Press, 2006). On society and culture in the 1920s and 1930s, see Mary Kay Vaughan, *Cultural Politics in Revolution: Teachers, Peasants, and Schools, 1930–1940* (Tucson: University of Arizona Press, 1997); Helen Delpar, *The Enormous Vogue of Things Mexican: Cultural Relations Between the United States and Mexico, 1920–1935* (Tuscaloosa: University of Alabama Press, 1992); and Mary Kay Vaughan and Stephen Lewis, eds., *The Eagle and the Virgin: Nation and Cultural Revolution in Mexico, 1920–1940* (Durham, NC: Duke University Press, 2005). The Cristero Rebellion is analyzed in Jennie Purnell, *Popular Movements and State Formation in Revolutionary Mexico: The Agraristas and Cristeros of Michoacán* (Durham, NC: Duke University Press, 1999), and Jean Meyer, *The Cristero Rebellion: The Mexican People Between Church and State, 1926–1929*, trans. Richard Southern (Cambridge: Cambridge University Press, 1976).

Much of the best scholarship on the Mexican Revolution is regional in character. See, for example, Gilbert M. Joseph, *Revolution from Without: Yucatán, Mexico, and the United States, 1880–1924* (Cambridge: Cambridge University Press, 1982); Christopher R. Boyer, *Becoming Campesinos: Politics, Identity, and Agrarian Struggle in Postrevolutionary Michoacán, 1920–1935* (Stanford, CA: Stanford University Press, 2003); Timothy Henderson, *The Worm in the Wheat: Rosalie Evans and Agrarian Struggle in the Puebla-Tlaxcala Region of Mexico, 1906–1927* (Durham, NC: Duke University Press, 1998); Stephen Lewis, *The Ambivalent Revolution: Forging State and Nation in Chiapas, 1910–1945* (Albuquerque: University of New Mexico Press, 2005); Mark Wasserman, *Persistent Oligarchs: Elites and Politics in Chihuahua, Mexico, 1910–1940* (Durham, NC: Duke University Press, 1993); and John Lear, *Workers, Neighbors, and Citizens: The Revolution in Mexico City* (Lincoln: University of Nebraska Press, 2001). Anthologies that contrast the revolution in different regions include Thomas Benjamin and Mark Wasserman, *Provinces of the Revolution: Essays on Regional Mexican History, 1910–1940* (Albuquerque: University of New Mexico Press, 1990); Gilbert M. Joseph and Daniel Nugent, eds., *Everyday Forms of State Formation: Revolution and the Negotiation of Rule in Modern Mexico* (Durham, NC: Duke University Press, 1994); and Jürgen Buchenau and William H. Beezley, *State Governors in the Mexican Revolution: Portraits in Conflict, Courage, and Corruption* (Lanham, MD: Rowman & Littlefield, forthcoming).

Apart from John W. F. Dulles, *Yesterday in Mexico: A Chronicle of the Revolution, 1919–1936* (Austin: University of Texas Press, 1961), the politics of the Obregón-Calles period from 1920 to 1935 have only recently become a subject of increasing study. See Jürgen Buchenau, *Plutarco Elías Calles and the Mexican*

Revolution (Lanham, MD: Rowman & Littlefield, 2007); and Nora Hamilton, *The Limits of State Authority: Post-Revolutionary Mexico* (Princeton, NJ: Princeton University Press, 1982).

Regarding the Cárdenas period, see Alan Knight, "Cardenismo: Juggernaut or Jalopy," *Journal of Latin American Studies* 26 (1994): 73–107; Friedrich E. Schuler, *Mexico between Hitler and Roosevelt: Mexican Foreign Relations in the Age of Lázaro Cárdenas, 1934–1940* (Albuquerque: University of New Mexico Press, 1998); Adrian A. Bantjes, *As If Jesus Walked on Earth: Cardenismo, Sonora, and the Mexican Revolution* (Wilmington, DE: SR Books, 1998); and Ben Fallaw, *Cárdenas Compromised: The Failure of Reform in Postrevolutionary Yucatán* (Durham, NC: Duke University Press, 2001). No good English-language biography of Lázaro Cárdenas has yet appeared, although William Cameron Townshend, *Lazaro Cardenas: Mexican Democrat* (Ann Arbor, MI: Wahr, 1952) is still helpful. A first-hand perspective written by the U.S. ambassador to Mexico is Josephus Daniels, *Shirt-Sleeve Diplomat* (Chapel Hill: University of North Carolina Press, 1947).

On Mexico during World War II, consult Stephen R. Niblo, *Mexico in the 1940s: Modernity, Politics, and Corruption* (Wilmington, DE: SR Books, 1999); Stephen R. Niblo, *War, Diplomacy, and Development: The United States and Mexico, 1938–1954* (Wilmington, DE: SR Books, 1995); María Emilia Paz, *Strategy, Security, and Spies: Mexico and the U.S. as Allies in World War Two* (University Park: Penn State University Press, 1997); and Daniel Newcomer, *Reconciling Modernity: Urban State Formation in the 1940s: León, Mexico* (Lincoln: University of Nebraska Press, 2004).

Chapter Five

The post–World War II period is a new frontier of historical scholarship. See Gilbert Joseph, Anne Rubenstein, and Eric Zolov, eds., *Fragments of a Golden Age: The Politics of Culture in Mexico Since 1940* (Durham, NC: Duke University Press, 2001); Kevin J. Middlebrook, *The Paradox of Revolution: Labor, the State, and Authoritarianism in Mexico* (Baltimore, MD: Johns Hopkins Press, 1995); and John W. Sherman, "The Mexican Miracle and Its Collapse," in *The Oxford History of Mexico*, eds. Michael C. Meyer and William H. Beezley, 575–98 (Oxford: Oxford University Press, 2000). Older studies include Howard Cline, *Mexico: Revolution to Evolution* (New York: Oxford University Press, 1963); Stanley R. Ross, *Is the Mexican Revolution Dead?* (New York: Knopf, 1966); and Raymond Vernon, *The Dilemma of Mexico's Development: The Roles of the Private and Public Sectors* (Cambridge, MA: Harvard University Press, 1963) Among first-person accounts, consult Irene Nicholson, *The X in Mexico: Growth Within Tradition* (London: Faber and Faber, 1965); Albert T'serstevens, *Mexico: Three-Storeyed Land*, trans. Alan Houghton Brodrick (Indianapolis, IN: Bobbs-Merrill, 1962); and Sydney A. Clark, *All the Best in Mexico* (New York: Dodd, Mead, 1956).

Mexico's cultural history since World War II has seen a recent outburst of scholarship. On Avándaro and the history of Mexican rock music, see Eric Zolov, *Refried Elvis: The Rise of the Mexican Counterculture* (Berkeley: University of California Press, 1999). Mexican popular and political culture is discussed in Anne Rubenstein, *Bad Language, Naked Ladies, and Other Threats to the Nation: A Political History of Comic Books in Mexico* (Durham, NC: Duke University Press, 1998); Jeffrey Pilcher, *Cantinflas and the Chaos of Mexican Modernity* (Wilmington, DE: SR Books, 2001), and Michael N. Miller, *Red, White, and Green: The Maturing of Mexicanidad* (El Paso: Texas Western Press, 1998). For a novel that portrays the process of institutionalization and corruption, see Carlos Fuentes, *The Death of Artemio Cruz* (New York: Farrar, Straus, Giroux, 1991). On tourism, consult Dina Berger, *The Development of Mexico's Tourism Industry: Pyramids by Day, Martinis by Night* (New York: Palgrave Macmillan, 2006).

Regarding the 1968 massacre, consult Elena Poniatowska, *Massacre in Mexico*, trans. Helen R. Lane (Independence: University of Missouri Press, 1992); Paco Ignacio Taibo II, *68*, trans. Donald Nicholson-Smith (New York: Seven Stories Press, 2004); and Elaine Carey, *Plaza of Sacrifices: Gender, Power, and Terror in 1968 Mexico* (Albuquerque: University of New Mexico Press, 2005).

For studies on the neopopulist 1970s and early 1980s, see Yoram Shapira, *Mexican Foreign Policy under Echeverría* (Beverly Hills, CA: Sage, 1978); Stanley Ross, ed., *Views across the Border* (Albuquerque: University of New Mexico Press, 1978); Merilee S. Grindle, *Bureaucrats, Politicians, and Peasants in Mexico: A Case Study in Public Policy* (Berkeley: University of California Press, 1977); and Samuel Schmidt, *The Deterioration of the Mexican Presidency* (Tucson: University of Arizona Press, 1991).

There is a rich literature concerning the economic crisis of 1982 and its aftermath as well as the process of globalization. See Stephen D. Morris, *Corruption and Politics in Contemporary Mexico* (Tuscaloosa: University of Alabama Press, 1991); Susan Eckstein, *The Poverty of Revolution: The State and the Urban Poor in Mexico* (Princeton, NJ: Princeton University Press, 1988); Jorge G. Castañeda and Robert A. Pastor, *Limits to Friendship: The United States and Mexico* (New York: Knopf, 1988); and Judith Adler Hellman, *Mexico in Crisis* (New York: Holmes and Meier, 1983). One particularly important protest and resistance movement is analyzed in Jeffrey Rubin, *Decentering the Regime: Ethnicity, Radicalism, and Democracy in Juchitán, Mexico* (Durham, NC: Duke University

Press, 1997). On the 1985 earthquake in Mexico City, see Elena Poniatowska, *Nothing, Nobody: The Voices of the Mexico City Earthquake*, trans. Aurora Camacho de Schmidt and Arthur Schmidt (Philadelphia, PA: Temple University Press, 1995); and Diane E. Davis, "Reverberations: Mexico City's 1985 Earthquake and the Transformation of the Capital," in *The Resilient City: How Modern Cities Recover From Disaster*, eds. Lawrence J. Vale and Thomas J. Campanella (Oxford: Oxford University Press, 2005), 255–80.

Scholars, journalists, and travelers have provided us with valuable perspectives on the lives of ordinary people in recent and contemporary Mexico. See Judith Adler Hellman, *Mexican Lives* (New York: The New Press, 1994); Larissa Adler Lomnitz, *Networks and Marginality: Life in a Mexican Shantytown* (New York: Academic Press, 1977); Velma García-Gorena, *Mothers and the Mexican Antinuclear Power Movement* (Tucson: University of Arizona Press, 1999); Oscar Lewis, *The Children of Sánchez: Autobiography of a Mexican Family* (New York: Random House, 1961); Alma Guillermoprieto, *Latin America: The Heart That Bleeds: Latin America Now* (New York: Vintage Books, 1995); Isabella Tree, *Sliced Iguana: Travels in Unknown Mexico* (London: Hamish Hamilton, 2001); and Sam Quinones, *True Tales from Another Mexico: The Lynch Mob, the Popsicle King, Chalino, and the Bronx* (Albuquerque: University of New Mexico Press, 2001).

On the Zapatista rebellion, see Shannan Mattiace, *To See with Two Eyes: Peasant Activism and Indian Autonomy in Chiapas* (Albuquerque: University of New Mexico Press, 2003); Neil Harvey, *The Chiapas Rebellion: The Struggle for Land and Democracy* (Durham, NC: Duke University Press, 1998); Nicholas P. Higgins, *Understanding the Chiapas Rebellion: Modernist Visions and the Invisible Indian* (Austin: University of Texas Press, 2004); and Lynn Stephen, *Zapata Lives! History and Cultural Politics in Southern Mexico* (Berkeley: University of California Press, 2002), among many others. A collection of EZLN manifestos is available in Subcomandante Marcos, *Our Word is Our Weapon: Selected Writings* (New York: Seven Stories Press, 2002).

Among the studies on globalization and Mexico in the NAFTA era, see Heather Williams, *Social Movements and Economic Transition: Markets and Distributive Conflict in Mexico* (New York: Cambridge University Press, 2001); Susan Kaufman Purcell, *Mexico in Transition: Implications for U.S. Policy* (New York: Council on Foreign Relations, 1988); Jorge G. Castañeda, *The Mexican Shock: Its Meaning for the United States* (New York: New Press, 1995); Sarah Babb, *Managing Mexico: Economists from Nationalism to Neoliberalism* (Princeton, NJ: Princeton University Press, 2001); and Kevin P. Gallagher, *Free Trade and the Environment: Mexico, NAFTA, and Beyond* (Stanford, CA: Stanford University Press, 2004).

On the recent history of the U.S.-Mexico border, see Miriam Davidson, *Lives on the Line: Dispatches from the U.S.-Mexico Border* (Tucson: University of Arizona Press, 2000).

Regarding democratization and the demise of the PRI as the ruling party, consult Daniel Levy and Kathleen Bruhn, *Mexico: The Struggle for Democratic Development*, 2nd ed. (Berkeley: University of California Press, 2006); Stephen D. Morris, *Political Reformism in Mexico: An Overview of Contempory Mexican Politics* (Boulder, CO: Lynn Rienner Publishers, 1995); Susan Kaufman Purcell and Luis Rubio, eds., *Mexico under Zedillo* (Boulder, CO: Lynn Rienner Publishers, 1998); Luis Rubio and Susan Kaufman Purcell, *Mexico under Fox* (Boulder, CO: Lynn Rienner Publishers, 2004); and Kevin Middlebrook, ed., *Dilemmas of Political Change in Mexico* (San Diego: UCSD Center for Mexican Studies, 2004).

Finally, Mexican immigration to the United States is the subject of a substantial literature. For an introduction to the topic, see Raúl Fernández, *A Century of Chicano History: Empire, Nations, and Migration* (New York: Routledge, 2003); Manuel Gonzales, *Mexicanos: A History of Mexicans in the United States* (Bloomington: Indiana University Press, 2000); and David G. Gutiérrez, *Between Two Worlds: Mexican Immigrants in the United States* (Wilmington, DE: SR Books, 1996). For a journalist's view, see Sam Quiñones, *Antonio's Gun and Delfino's Dream: True Tales of Mexican Migration* (Albuquerque: University of New Mexico Press, 2007).

⚘ Glossary ⚘

alcabala sales tax imposed by the Spanish Crown

alcaldes mayores regional leaders who answered to the Spanish viceroy

Alhóndiga de Granaditas granary in the city of Guanajuato

Asamblea Popular de los Pueblos de Oaxaca APPO, or Popular Assembly of the Peoples of Oaxaca

audiencia legislative and judicial body in Spanish colonial America

Aztlán legendary land north of the Aztecs from which they believed they came south to Mexico

braceros wartime guestworkers in the U.S.

cabildo abierto open city council at the time of Independence in Latin America

caciques local bosses

campesino peasant

Casa del Obrero Mundial House of the World's Worker, an anarcho-syndicalist labor union affiliated with the Industrial Workers of the World during the Mexican Revolution

caudillos regional warlords

Chan Santa Cruz Cult of the Speaking Cross in Yucatán

charro cowboy

Chichimeca assorted nomadic communities in northern Mesoamerica

Chichén Itzá the most powerful city in Yucatán in the eleventh century

chinampas floating gardens for irrigation in the Valley of Mexico before the conquest

Ciudadela Mexico City's armory

ciudades perdidas "lost cities," or shantytowns

clientelism the practice of using ties of family, marriage, and friendship to forge important economic and political networks

cofradías religious fraternities

Confederación Regional Obrera Mexicana CROM or Mexican Regional Workers' Confederation

Confederación de Trabajadores Mexicanos CTM or Confederation of Mexican Workers

Consejo Nacional Campesino CNC or National Campesino Council

corregidores regional leaders who answered to the Spanish viceroy

Cortes de Cádiz set up in Cádiz in 1812 to draft Spain's first liberal constitution

creole a Spaniard born in the New World

dedazo fingerpoint (slang for choosing one's presidential successor)

día de Guadalupe December 12, the celebration in honor of the Virgin of Guadalupe

Ejército Zapatista de Liberación Nacional EZLN or Zapatista Army of National Liberation

ejército trigarante the Army of the Three Guarantees: *independencia unión*, and *religión*

ejidos communal land

encomenderos land-grant holders

encomienda a land grant entitling the owner to dominion over the indigenous community in exchange for bringing Christianity to Indians

Federales federal army

Frente Democrático Nacional FDN or National Democratic Front

fueros special privileges that established separate systems of jurisdiction for the army, the Church, and the indigenous population

gachupines derisive term for Spaniards

gente alta the "high" people or elite, property owners

gente decente the "decent" people, or middle class, including both professionals and artisans

gente humilde the "humble" people, or poor, including the urban workers and beggars

gracias al sacar a purchased certificate claiming the holder to be a Christian of pure Spanish descent

granaderos paramilitary riot police

Grito de Dolores the "Cry of Dolores," uttered by Miguel Hidalgo y Costilla

hacienda a great agricultural estate in private (Spanish) hands

hidalgos derived from the phrase *hijo de algo* or son of something; younger sons of Spanish aristocrats

hombres de maíz people of corn; indigenous Mesoamericans

Huitzilopochtli bloodthirsty Aztec god

los imperialistas a group of Mexican advisers to Maximilian steeped in the liberal policies of modern French thought

informe national address given by the president to Congress every September 1

jefe político formal political official such as the mayor

leva military draft

léperos lepers; a derogatory term widely used to describe beggars

Malintzín or **La Malinche** the translator of Hernan Cortés, her name stands for treasonous behavior

malinchismo the act of a Mexican who has turned his or her back on the fatherland

mariachi Mexican music or band

maquiladoras partial-assembly plants near the U.S. border

Maximato 1928–1955, the era of puppet presidents under Calles as the Jefe Máximo

mayorazgo the entail, or concession, necessary to obtain noble status or pass wealth from one generation to the next

mestizo a descendant of mixed parentage: Spanish and indigenous or African

Mexicanidad Mexicanness

milpa raised field

Moctezuma II ruler of the Aztec Empire in 1502

moderados moderate Liberals of the 1840s

Movimiento Armado Revolucionario MAR or Armed Revolutionary Movement

la noche triste the sad night, July 1, 1520, when at least 450 Spaniards died during the escape from the Aztec capital

obraje textile sweatshop

oidores judges placed by the Spanish Crown

palenques runaway-slave communities

Partido Acción Nacional PAN or the conservative National Action Party

Partido Liberal Mexicano PLM or Mexican Liberal Party

Partido Nacional Revolucionario PNR or National Revolutionary Party

Partido de la Revolución Mexicana PRM or Party of the Mexican Revolution

Partido de la Revolución Democrática PRD or the left-leaning Party of the Democratic Revolution

Partido Revolucionario Institucional PRI or the Institutional Revolutionary Party

patronato real kingly patronage

pelado a bum (derogatory)

peninsulares native-born Spaniards in Mexico

Petróleos Mexicanos PEMEX, the national oil company

Los Pinos the presidential palace in Mexico City

pipiltín Aztec priest-rulers

Popol Vuh Maya creation myth

Porfiriato the age of the rule of Porfirio Díaz

presidios colonial garrisons

pueblos rural towns with a mix of indigenous people and mestizos

puros radical Liberals of the 1840s

Quetzalcóatl the plumed serpent, chief Toltec god

reconquista the age of reconquest of Iberia from the Moors

repartimiento the institution of requiring indigenous communities to contribute a percentage of laborers to nearby Spanish authorities

rurales the brutal rural police in late nineteenth-century Mexico

soldaderas female soldiers

subdelegados intendants, many of whom were born in Spain, who replaced creole corregidores

telenovela soap opera

Tenochtitlán the Aztec capital

Teotihuacán major city-state in the Valley of Mexico

Tezcatlipoca Toltec militaristic god

Tlaxcaltecos an enemy civilization of the Aztecs favored by them for human sacrifice

Tribunal Federal Electoral federal elections jury

Zócalo the central square of Mexico City

❧ Index ❧

Mexican Mosaic: A Brief History of Mexico
Developmental editor: Andrew J. Davidson
Copy editor and Production editor: Lucy Herz
Proofreader: Claudia Siler
Cartographer: Jason Casanova, Pegleg Graphics
Cover designer: Christopher Calvetti
Indexer: Margie Towery Indexing

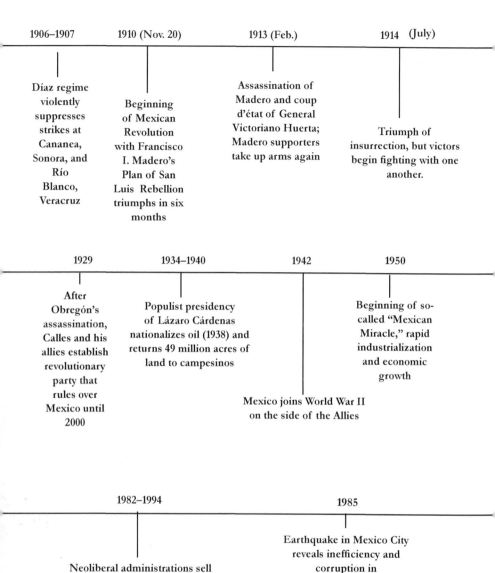

1906–1907	1910 (Nov. 20)	1913 (Feb.)	1914 (July)

Díaz regime violently suppresses strikes at Cananea, Sonora, and Río Blanco, Veracruz

Beginning of Mexican Revolution with Francisco I. Madero's Plan of San Luis Rebellion triumphs in six months

Assassination of Madero and coup d'état of General Victoriano Huerta; Madero supporters take up arms again

Triumph of insurrection, but victors begin fighting with one another.

1929	1934–1940	1942	1950

After Obregón's assassination, Calles and his allies establish revolutionary party that rules over Mexico until 2000

Populist presidency of Lázaro Cárdenas nationalizes oil (1938) and returns 49 million acres of land to campesinos

Beginning of so-called "Mexican Miracle," rapid industrialization and economic growth

Mexico joins World War II on the side of the Allies

1982–1994	1985

Neoliberal administrations sell off state-owned industries and end government regulation of industry and trade

Earthquake in Mexico City reveals inefficiency and corruption in government response